Paul's Gospel and Mission

THE OUTLOOK FROM HIS LETTER TO THE ROMANS

Arland J. Hultgren

FORTRESS PRESS   **PHILADELPHIA**

Library of Congress Cataloging in Publication Data

Hultgren, Arland J.
  Paul's gospel and mission.

  Includes indexes.
  1. Paul, the Apostle, Saint. 2. Bible. N.T. Romans—
Criticism, interpretation, etc. 3. Bible, N.T.
Epistles of Paul—Theology. I. Title.
BS2506.H85 1985   227'.106   85-4430
ISBN 0-8006-1871-8

1731A85   Printed in the United States of America   1-1871

To
Peter
Stephen
Kristina

Contents

Preface

The most decisive event in Paul's life was the appearance of the risen Christ to him, which he mentions three times in his letters (1 Cor. 9:1; 15:8; Gal. 1:15–16). In that event, which determined his life and dominated his consciousness, he was commissioned with the gospel and his mission as an apostle. Throughout the rest of his life he continued to give thought to the gospel and his mission, and he expressed his thoughts in his letters. If we are to understand other aspects of his thought and activities, and if we are to understand his letters, we need to understand first of all Paul's reflection on his gospel and mission as a driving force.

But an attempt to probe Paul is beset with problems. His letters address different issues, and it is likely that over time, and during his proclamation, his facing of opponents, and his writing to the various communities — and perhaps in still other circumstances — Paul's views became clearer and were developed more fully. That is to say, what was essentially an orientation or outlook from the beginning became expressed more explicitly later.

The present study is based primarily on passages in Paul's Letter to the Romans, which is taken here to be the last letter of Paul and the final literary expression of his thinking. It seeks to make connections with Paul's statements elsewhere in his earlier letters as well. It is demonstrated frequently, where possible, that there was an essential coherence to his thinking about the gospel and his own mission throughout his years as an apostle, but this coherence came to its fullest expression in his final letter.

The study has been carried on within the context of teaching courses in the exegesis of the Pauline letters, particularly Romans, in a theological seminary. The chapters deal with particular issues that arise in connection with exegesis as one tries to carry on the complementary tasks of offering a theological summation from exegesis, and providing a theological perspective for exegesis. The two must inevitably go together within what has commonly been called the "hermeneutical circle."

Here I do not deal with all aspects of Pauline theology, nor do I provide extensive commentary on any one letter. Rather I focus on the issues of Paul's gospel and mission, as these are given theological expression in his letters, particularly Romans. These issues have been discussed in the classroom, in congregational settings, and in countless conversations with students, colleagues in teaching and parish ministry, and other friends.

The interpretation of Paul's gospel and mission presented here is informed by the work of other interpreters, but it goes its own way as well. The interpreter of Paul is obliged, as far as possible, "to think the thoughts" of the apostle himself, as these are expressed in his letters. But interpretation is more than mere repetition. It involves an asking of questions, posing tentative answers, and working out the details through both an engagement with the actual texts and in a theological engagement that draws out the consequences of what is explicitly written. As it has been said about science—that "it is not a collection of facts, but what one makes of the facts"—the same can be said of historical and literary interpretation. An interpretation is obliged to make something of the facts. The interpreter is accountable to the canons of coherence and consistency; what is said must cohere with the actual data provided in the texts, and it must also provide a picture that has an integral consistency among its parts. The interpreter therefore takes risks and makes proposals that are subject to critique. And interpretation is then an ongoing task in light of new questions and ever new perspectives.

Paul's reflections on the gospel and his own mission are important to understand for anyone who is interested in the historical reconstruction of Christian origins. But as a consequence of the study of his thinking, the conviction may well arise, and rightly so, that his views are essential for doing theology today and for the church's mission. Like those in the past, people of our own generation and those to come can profit from a study of Paul. It is therefore fitting that — with a view to the future — this work be dedicated to three young persons, my children: Peter, Stephen, and Kristina.

Luther Northwestern Theological Seminary   A. J. H.
St. Paul, Minnesota

Abbreviations

Pseudepigrapha

Apoc. Bar.	Apocalypse of Baruch (2 Baruch)
Pss. Sol.	Psalms of Solomon
T. Benj.	Testament of Benjamin
T. Judah	Testament of Judah
T. Zeb.	Testament of Zebulon

Dead Sea Scrolls

1QM	*War Scroll*
1QS	*Manual of Discipline*

Rabbinic Texts

m. Sanh.	*Mishnah, Sanhedrin*
m. Yoma	*Mishnah, Yoma*

Josephus

Ant.	*Jewish Antiquities*
J.W.	*The Jewish War*

Philo

Cher.	*On the Cherubim (De Cherubim)*
Deus Imm.	*On the Unchangeableness of God (Quod Deus Immutabilis sit)*
In Flaccum	*To Flaccus*

| *Legatio ad Gaium* | *On the Embassy to Gaius (De Legatione ad Gaium)* |
| *Vit. Mos.* | *On the Life of Moses (De Vita Mosis)* |

JOURNALS, REFERENCE WORKS, AND SERIALS

ACNT	Augsburg Commentary on the New Testament
AJA	*American Journal of Archaeology*
ANF	*The Ante-Nicene Fathers,* ed. Alexander Roberts and James Donaldson, 9 vols. (New York: Christian Literature Company, 1890)
APOT	*Apocrypha and Pseudepigrapha of the Old Testament in English,* ed. R. H. Charles, 2 vols. (New York: Oxford Univ. Press, 1913)
ASRV	American Standard Revised Version
BAGD	W. Bauer, W. F. Arndt, F. W. Gingrich, *A Greek-English Lexicon of the New Testament and Other Early Christian Literature,* 2d ed., rev. F. W. Gingrich and F. W. Danker (Chicago: Univ. of Chicago Press, 1979)
BDF	F. Blass, A. Debrunner, and R. W. Funk, *A Greek Grammar of the New Testament and Other Early Christian Literature* (Chicago: Univ. of Chicago Press, 1961)
BEvT	Beiträge zur evangelischen Theologie
Bib	*Biblica*
ConBNT	Coniectanea biblica, New Testament
EKKNT	Evangelisch-katholischer Kommentar zum Neuen Testament
EncJud	*Encyclopaedia Judaica,* ed. C. Roth and G. Widoger, 16 vols. (New York: Macmillan Co., 1971)
EvT	*Evangelische Theologie*
ExpTim	*Expository Times*
FRLANT	Forschungen zur Religion und Literatur des Alten und Neuen Testaments
HDR	Harvard Dissertations in Religion
HNT	Handbuch zum Neuen Testament
HNTC	Harper's New Testament Commentary
HTKNT	Herders theologischer Kommentar zum Neuen Testament

HTR	*Harvard Theological Review*
ICC	International Critical Commentary
IDB	*Interpreter's Dictionary of the Bible*, ed. G. Buttrick, 4 vols. (Nashville: Abingdon Press, 1962)
IDBSup	*Interpreter's Dictionary of the Bible — Supplementary Volume*, ed. K. Crim (Nashville: Abingdon Press, 1976)
Int	*Interpretation*
JB	Jerusalem Bible
JBL	*Journal of Biblical Literature*
JBLMS	Journal of Biblical Literature Monograph Series
JSNT	*Journal for the Study of the New Testament*
JSNTSup	Journal for the Study of the New Testament Supplement Series
JTS	*Journal of Theological Studies*
KJV	King James Version
LCC	Library of Christian Classics
LCL	Loeb Classical Library
LXX	The Septuagint
MeyerK	Kritisch-exegetischer Kommentar über das Neue Testament ("Meyer Kommentar")
MNTC	Moffatt New Testament Commentary
MT	Masoretic Text
NAB	New American Bible
NCB	New Century Bible
NEB	New English Bible
NIV	New International Version
NovT	*Novum Testamentum*
NovTSup	Novum Testamentum, Supplements
NTAbh	Neutestamentliche Abhandlungen
NTS	*New Testament Studies*
PWSup	Supplement to *Paulys Realencyclopädia der classischen Altertumswissenschaft*, ed. G. Wissowa, 15 vols. to date (Stuttgart: A. Druckenmüller, 1903–)
RSV	Revised Standard Version
SBLDS	Society of Biblical Literature Dissertation Series
SBLMS	Society of Biblical Literature Monograph Series
SBLSBS	Society of Biblical Literature Sources for Biblical Study

SBLSCS	Society of Biblical Literature Septuagint and Cognate Studies
SBT	Studies in Biblical Theology
SEÅ	*Svensk Exegetisk Årsbok*
SNTSMS	Society for New Testament Studies Monograph Series
ST	*Studia theologica*
Str-B	H. Strack and P. Billerbeck, *Kommentar zum Neuen Testament aus Talmud und Midrasch*, 6 vols. (Munich: C. H. Beck'sche, 1922–1961)
TDNT	*Theological Dictionary of the New Testament*, ed. G. Kittel and G. Friedrich, 10 vols. (Grand Rapids: Wm. B. Eerdmans, 1964–76)
TEV	Today's English Version
TF	Theologische Forschung
TLZ	*Theologische Literaturzeitung*
TNTC	Tyndale New Testament Commentary
UNT	Untersuchungen zum Neuen Testament
VD	*Verbum Domini*
WMANT	Wissenschaftliche Monographien zum Alten und Neuen Testament
WUNT	Wissenschaftliche Untersuchungen zum Neuen Testament
ZNW	*Zeitschrift für die neutestamentliche Wissenschaft*
ZTK	*Zeitschrift für Theologie und Kirche*

1. Paul's Gospel and Theology

Interpreters of Paul have sought to find the center of his thinking, an axis from which all the other spokes of his thought and proclamation radiate outward, and by which his letters can be understood. The task is complicated. Is the "center" of his thinking to be found in a particular theological perspective? Is it to be found in his experience of being confronted by the risen Lord, of which he speaks on occasion (1 Cor. 15:8; Gal. 1:16; cf. 1 Cor. 9:1)? Is it to be found in his delineation of the Christian life as being essentially a life "in Christ"?

THE QUEST FOR AN ASSESSMENT

Since the Reformation, many interpreters have claimed that the coherent center is to be found in Paul's doctrine of justification by faith. Paul is then thought of primarily as a theologian and, indeed, as the most profound theologian of the first century. But not all interpreters in modern times have agreed with that assessment. Was Paul, after all, primarily a theologian? In a book published in 1895 Adolf Deissmann called into question this picture of Paul. Deissmann gave attention to the form of Paul's letters, saw them as occasional works addressed to his contemporaries, and concluded that in no instance can they be described as theological essays. He wrote:

> The letters of Paul are not so much sources for the theology, or even for the religion, of the period, as simply for the personal religion of Paul as an individual; it is only by a literary misconception that they are looked upon as the documents of "Paulinism." The result of their criticism from the standpoint of the history of religion can be nothing more than a sketch of the character of Paul the letter-writer, and not the system of Paul the epistolographer; what speaks to us in the letters is

his faith, not his dogmatics; his morality, not his ethics; his hopes, not his eschatology—here and there, no doubt, in the faltering speech of theology. The early Christian epistles are the monuments of a religion which was gradually accommodating itself to external conditions, which had established itself in the world, which received its stimulus less in the closet than in the church, and which was on the way to express itself in liturgy and as *doctrine*.[1]

According to this view, the letters of Paul reflect the faith, morality, and hopes of the apostle "in the faltering speech of theology" at best. Paul was not primarily a theologian but an apostle, preacher, and letter writer working within the context of issues confronting him and his congregations. He did not have a theological, much less dogmatic, system from which he spoke and wrote. Any attempt to describe a "theology" of Paul is therefore to beg a question methodologically. To speak of a "Pauline theology" is an anachronism.

The assertions of Deissmann must be taken seriously. Moreover, it has been realized increasingly in recent years that Paul's letters are not theological essays; they are occasional pieces written to congregations founded by Paul or, in the case of Romans, to be visited by him. In recent times J. Christiaan Beker has insisted that a distinction must be made between "contingency and coherence" in Paul's letters. Granting that there is a "coherence" to Paul's thinking, nevertheless:

> The coherent center of the gospel is never an abstraction removed from its "address" and audience; it cannot be a *depositum fidei* or doctrinal abstraction that as a universal, timeless substance is to be poured into every conceivable situation regardless of historical circumstance. In other words, the truth of the gospel is bound up with its contingency and historical concreteness. Particularity and occasionality do not constitute a contamination of Paul's "pure thought"; rather, they serve to make the truth of the gospel the effective word of God.[2]

For all their differences, both Deissmann and Beker (and others could be included as well) have insisted on the "occasional" character of the letters. Paul was an apostle, preacher, and letter writer who spoke to particular audiences of the first century. He was not a theologian who worked apart from particular contexts; he did not set out to produce a "timeless" theology.

PAUL'S LETTERS:
GOSPEL AND THEOLOGY

As important as it is to make this point, it should be recognized, however, that every theologian works in a context. The great "moments" in theology have usually been instances of crisis for believing communities. In these moments of crisis there is a close association between faith and theology, so that the two overlap in ways that they normally do not. One can cite here within the history of Israel certain formative figures – the Deuteronomist, the writers who responded to the exile in Babylonia, and the apocalyptists; and in subsequent history one can cite Paul himself, the early Church Fathers and Apologists, Martin Luther, and others. In each of these instances the formative figures were persons of great faith and insight, and their writings were "occasional," but these persons were not any the less theologians. Religious fervor and theology are intertwined in their writings to a rare degree. William Wrede recognized this long ago in the case of Paul when he wrote that Paul's religion and theology can hardly be separated: "The religion of the apostle is theological through and through: his theology is his religion."[3]

Theology is always contextual, and what makes Paul and other major formative theologians stand out in the history of the biblical and postbiblical tradition is that the form of their works reflects the peculiar needs of their momentous contexts; form follows function. What makes Paul different from later Christian theologians is not that he was an occasional and contextual writer, while later theologians have not been. What makes Paul different is that he expressed his theology in letters and apparently did not reflect self-consciously on himself as a theologian who tried to give a coherent presentation of the Christian faith. In this respect Paul can be considered closer to Luther as theologian than to John Calvin. Luther was certainly a theologian, but his writings were usually occasional, not "systematic."[4] Calvin, on the other hand, wrote his *Institutes* more self-consciously as a theologian. One can debate the strengths and weaknesses of each as a theologian, but that each was a theologian is not disputed. And that Paul was a theologian then need not be debated, for he most certainly was such.

The letters of Paul convey his gospel, paraenesis (ethical advice), greetings, personal plans, and more. They are not theological essays. Yet they are the writings of one who had "seen the Lord" (1 Cor. 9:1) and who had been appointed apostle to the gentiles or nations (Rom. 11:13; Gal. 2:7). Paul had experienced a critical moment in the appearance of the risen Lord to him, and in the aftermath of that crisis he reflected on the ways of God with the world, inhabited by Jews and gentiles, in light of the revelation of God's Son. Paul the Pharisee became Paul the apostle and theologian. As summarized by Joseph A. Fitzmyer, the "revelation" of the risen Lord to Paul (Gal. 1:16) had at least three effects on Paul's thinking: (1) it impressed Paul with the divine action for the salvation of humanity; (2) it taught him to rethink the matter of messiahship, so that the previously unheard of concept of a crucified Messiah became central to this thinking; and (3) it impressed him with a new view of salvation history, so that now he realized that the messianic age had already begun with the death and resurrection of Jesus as the Messiah, although it will be realized fully only at the Parousia.[5]

Paul does not of course speak of his "theology" but of his "gospel" (Rom. 2:16; 2 Cor. 4:3; Gal. 1:11; 2:2; 1 Thess. 1:5).[6] But that he was a theologian of immense stature cannot be denied. His letters contain chiefly "first order language" of religious discourse. That is the language of proclamation, faith, doxology, and prayer. His letters are often then "unsystematic" when measured by the standards of later theological "second order language." Frequently they contain inconsistencies and "outbursts" (often doxological). But they also contain sustained theological treatments of particular themes, as in the case of Romans 9 – 11, in which Paul takes up the question of the salvation of Israel in the face of the latter's overwhelming rejection of the gospel. And even in other instances – as when Paul speaks of the righteousness of God, the meaning of Christ's death and resurrection, and the sacraments, to name only a few topics – it is clear that Paul has given considerable theological reflection. The letters do not then always speak "in the faltering speech of theology" but are permeated at many places with profound theological reflection.

As interpreters have generally recognized, there is a "Pauline theology" which comes to expression in the letters and which can be described in its essentials. *That* it can be described is not debated; *how* one describes it remains the problem. It is generally conceded today that it would be inappropriate and misleading to employ a systematic arrangement of topics from subsequent theology — used for pedagogical purposes in dogmatics — as the basis for an orderly presentation (e.g., revelation, God, Christ, sin, redemption, Spirit, church, sacraments, last things, etc.). One would then miss the very spirit and dynamic of Paul's theology and proclamation, in which all things tend to be interwoven. On the other hand, it is clear that Paul did reflect on major topics of Christian theology. His doctrinal teachings were expressed in the contexts of proclamation, response to questions, or debate, and they were undoubtedly sharpened by the contingencies of the moment, but that does not mean that his thought lacked a basic coherence. Günther Bornkamm has asserted that Paul's theology is presented in the way it is because his theology has a peculiar nature and subject matter. It is dominated by the encounter between God, humankind, and the world.[7] Paul did not take up for himself the vocation of treating "stock themes" of Christian theology or presenting an account of "the Christian faith" in a coherent manner in his letters. His vocation was that of an apostle and preacher, a proclaimer of the gospel. Even in those moments at which he was most clearly a theologian he did not thereby cease to be a proclaimer of the gospel. The gospel he received gave impetus to theological reflection, and his theological reflections were expressed through his letters to aid his readers in understanding the gospel and its implications for their own lives. His treatments of such matters as sin, baptism, and justification, for example, indicate that he thought deeply about the action of God toward the world. He could therefore *declare* that action, and that was to proclaim the gospel. But he could also *treat* that action thoughtfully, and to do so was to do theology. Both activities were necessary.

We do not have the whole of Paul's theology, nor even all the letters that he wrote.[8] We have only those letters that have been transmitted to us through the church from the apostolic age to the present, and not all of those attributed to Paul can be taken as genuine. Along with many other studies of Paul today,[9] this one accepts only seven letters in the New Testament to be indisputably genuine: Romans, 1 and 2

Corinthians, Galatians, Philippians, 1 Thessalonians, and Philemon. Given the situation of relatively few resources, and knowing that these do not contain all that Paul taught and wrote, any presentation of Paul's theology can be only fragmentary. The problem of finding a coherence to it is compounded by the fact that his letters were written at various times and in different settings — both for him and his readers. It is also possible that certain shifts took place in his thinking.[10] Moreover, since there are inconsistencies here and there, the interpreter is forced to make decisions on how much weight to place on certain passages. In such cases it seems appropriate that greater weight should be given to those places in Paul's letters at which a sustained argument — a more reflective, theological presentation — is made. Contexts must be explored, and sporadic pronouncements called forth by the needs of the moment must be seen over against those passages that exhibit a more sustained presentation that coheres with other emphases in the letters. This calls for judgment and theological critique, and interpreters will inevitably differ on what is significant, but there is no other way to proceed. The alternative is silence.

The present study is not intended to be a complete theology of Paul. It is devoted to themes that can be considered significant — even central — to Paul, and in light of which other themes can be related. The themes selected have to do with essentials of Paul's gospel and mission, and themes on which Paul gave theological reflection. Four basic themes are explored. First, how has God disclosed himself to the world in light of the Christ event? The important theme of the righteousness of God is explored in chapter 2. That the theme is considered significant — perhaps even pivotal — for Paul can be attested by the sheer amount of attention it has been given in recent years — probably more than any other single theme. Second, what has God done through the death and resurrection of Jesus Christ? Attention centers in chapter 3 on Rom. 3:21–26 as the most significant treatment by Paul on this matter, and then other passages are explored which have to do with the divine action through Christ as well. Third, what are the effects or benefits for humankind that have accrued through the divine action? The theme of justification is explored in chapter 4. One could of course treat other metaphors and themes in Paul (e.g., reconciliation, redemption, etc.), but the language of justification is the most frequent soteriological metaphor in Paul, and the theme of justification is undoubtedly the most lasting legacy in this area from Paul. But justification has been treated generally under the topic of "justification by faith." In this chapter the latter is set aside, and justification is examined within the broader scope of Pauline theology and its treatment in Rom. 5:12–21, and then the theme of justification by faith is treated in light of the previous discussion. Our contention is that justification language is used by Paul in two contexts. This has been missed in previous scholarship, leading to a one-sided presentation. Finally, how did Paul conceive of his mission? How could he say, as he does in Rom. 15:23, that his mission in the East had been concluded, when he had of course not evangelized every community or person there, so that he could now go on to Rome, Spain, and perhaps beyond? The final chapter therefore takes up the question of how Paul thought about his mission as apostle to the nations, integrating the discussion with the earlier chapters of this study.

What follows is based primarily on Paul's letter to the Romans. Since that is so, a statement should be made concerning the author's assessment of the place and function of this letter in Paul's work. From the letter itself certain things emerge clearly. Paul intends to go to Rome (1:10, 15) — a church that he had not founded — to fulfill hopes he has had for years (15:23). But that visit will take place only after a visit to Jerusalem for the purpose of delivering to that church a collection from the churches that he had founded (15:25–27). When he comes to Rome, the apostle expects to have a good reception (15:29) and to enjoy the company of the Romans for a while (15:24, 32). From there he intends to proceed to Spain (15:24, 28), and he expects to do so with the support (both spiritual and financial[11]) of the Roman congregation.[12] Paul appeals to the Roman Christians even now for their prayers (15:30), as he prepares to go to Jerusalem, that he will be safe (15:31a) and that his collection will be accepted by the saints in Jerusalem as a symbol of unity with the churches he has founded (15:31b).

Interpreters have raised questions concerning the purposes of Romans in light of the data. Three basic positions can be seen to emerge among them, which can be called "minimal," "maximal," and "mediating" positions. The "minimal" position does not speculate beyond the data given in the letter. Paul seeks support for his planned trip to Spain, so he presented his gospel in order to announce his forthcoming visit and to establish a relationship with the church there.[13] The "maximal" position is that, while this was the case, nevertheless Paul had other purposes in mind. As in the case of other letters, in which Paul spoke to live issues in the congregations addressed, so he sought to speak to issues at Rome (e.g., the question of obedience to governing authorities in 13:1-7 and relationships between the "strong" and the "weak" in 14 and 15).[14] The "mediating" position falls somewhere between the other two. Building upon the "minimal" position, various interpreters have claimed that more can be said without going so far as to say that Romans is to be assessed specifically in light of the purposes of the other letters (i.e., that Paul's agenda was primarily to address live issues, even though some issues arise in chapters 13–15; that fact does not explain most of what appears in chapters 1–12). Paul's purpose was of course to announce his forthcoming visit to Rome and to tell of his plans to go to Spain. But beyond that, he had the visit to Jerusalem in mind. He therefore summarized some of his themes from earlier letters for some purpose. Suggestions as to what this purpose was include: (1) the preparation of a "last will and testament" of his teaching in case his career should come to an end;[15] (2) the winning of solidarity with himself in the Roman church in relation to the Jerusalem church;[16] or (3) the preparation of what he would say to the church at Jerusalem on his arrival there.[17]

What has been called here the "mediating" position has various specific proposals, but common to all is the view that in this letter Paul moves toward a comprehensive theological statement.[18] Bornkamm has stated the matter explicitly: this letter "summarizes and develops the most important themes and thoughts of the Pauline message and theology" and "elevates his theology above the moment of definite situations and conflicts into the sphere of the eternally and universally valid."[19]

The position taken in this study is a "mediating" one as well. It is assumed—along with various interpreters—that Romans was Paul's last letter.[20] Paul hints that his forthcoming visit to Jerusalem with the collection might not turn out to be favorable (15:31). If that should be the case, the repercussions could spell disaster for his apostleship in other churches not founded by him, including the church of Rome, and his mission to Spain with Roman support would be in jeopardy. That would be particularly so, since the Roman church consisted in part of Jewish Christians,[21] for whom the church in Jerusalem would have had a special regard and authority. Paul's purpose in writing to the church in Rome was, then, more than an announcement of his forthcoming visit. He has to present to that church the gospel that he proclaims so that even if his reception in Jerusalem should turn out to be unfavorable, he would nevertheless find support in Rome for his intended mission. Paul could not think of his mission as idiosyncratic, nor could he think of his own churches (from which he could of course expect support) as separate from others. The church at Rome, not founded by him, was an important center by the time Paul wrote, and he had to have it as an ally in his western mission. But in order to win that support (especially if the Jerusalem church was unaccepting), it was necessary for Paul to present the essentials of his gospel there. Therefore, as various interpreters have shown, Paul re-presented in Romans various themes that had appeared in his earlier letters, but in a way that was more seasoned and comprehensive.[22] He raised his earlier affirmations — often worked out in polemical contexts — to a more universal level. It has been said, then, that Romans has the character of a "summary of Pauline proclamation."[23] Romans is not a "compendium of Christian doctrine," but it does sum up major themes of Pauline proclamation and theology. The study of Paul's gospel and mission cannot be limited to Romans, but it is appropriate to use Romans as a basic document for such a study, because of its character as a summary of the essentials of his proclamation and theology.

NOTES

1. Adolf Deissmann, *Bible Studies*, 2d ed. (Edinburgh: T. & T. Clark, 1903), 58. The first German edition appeared in 1895.

2. J. Christiaan Beker, *Paul the Apostle: The Triumph of God in Life and Thought* (Philadelphia: Fortress Press, 1980), 24.

3. William Wrede, *Paul* (Boston: American Unitarian Association, 1908), 76.

4. So it has been said that Luther's academic lectures, for example, were "preached dogmatics." See David W. Lotz, "The Proclamation of the Word in Luther's Thought," *Word & World* 3 (1983):353.

5. Joseph A. Fitzmyer, *Pauline Theology: A Brief Sketch* (Englewood Cliffs, N.J.: Prentice-Hall, 1967), 8–11.

6. The term "theology" existed already in classical Greece. Cf. Plato *Republic* 379A5, where the term *theologia* is used.

7. Günther Bornkamm, *Paul* (New York: Harper & Row, 1971), 118.

8. So, for example, 2 Cor. 2:4 refers to a letter otherwise apparently unknown.

9. Bornkamm, *Paul*, 241–43; Norman Perrin, *The New Testament: An Introduction* (New York: Harcourt Brace Jovanovich, 1974), 97–117; E. P. Sanders, *Paul and Palestinian Judaism: A Comparison of Patterns of Religion* (Philadelphia: Fortress Press, 1977), 431; Beker, *Paul the Apostle*, 3; and Helmut Koester, *Introduction to the New Testament* (Philadelphia: Fortress Press, 1982), 2:52.

10. Cf. Charles H. Buck and Greer Taylor, *Saint Paul: A Study of the Development of His Thought* (New York: Charles Scribner's Sons, 1969).

11. The verb *propempō* in Rom. 15:24 means to "help on one's journey with food, money, by arranging for companions, means of travel, etc.," BAGD, 709.

12. Although one can speak of a Roman "church" or "congregation," it has been suggested that this church may have been made up of at least three "house churches" (Rom. 16:5, 14, 15) designated as one church; so Abraham J. Malherbe, *Social Aspects of Early Christianity* (Baton Rouge, La.: Louisiana State Univ. Press, 1977), 70.

13. Charles H. Dodd, *The Epistle of Paul to the Romans*, MNTC (New York: Harper & Brothers, 1932), xxiv–xxvi.

14. Major proponents here are Paul Minear, *The Obedience of Faith*, SBT 2/19 (London: SCM Press, 1971) and Karl P. Donfried, "False Presuppositions in the Study of Romans," in *The Romans Debate*, ed. Karl Donfried (Minneapolis: Augsburg Pub. House, 1977), 120–48. What is called a "maximal" position here is called the "situational theory" by Robert Jewett, "Romans as an Ambassadorial Letter," *Int.* 36 (1982):5–6.

15. Günther Bornkamm, "The Letter to the Romans as Paul's Last Will and Testament," in *The Romans Debate*, ed. Donfried, 17–31; idem, *Paul*, 88–96; Werner G. Kümmel, *Introduction to the New Testament*, rev. ed. (Nashville: Abingdon Press, 1975), 311–14; and Ulrich Wilckens, *Der Brief an die Römer*, EKKNT 6 (Köln: Benziger; Neukirchen-Vluyn: Neukirchener, 1978–82), 1:47–48.

16. Ernst Käsemann, *Commentary on Romans* (Grand Rapids: Wm. B.

Eerdmans, 1980), 402–5; C. E. B. Cranfield, *A Critical and Exegetical Commentary on the Epistle to the Romans,* ICC (Edinburgh: T. & T. Clark, 1975–79), 823.

17. Jacob Jervell, "The Letter to Jerusalem," in *The Romans Debate,* ed. Donfried, 61–74.

18. Of course Romans does not contain a totally comprehensive treatment, since some topics (e.g., the Lord's Supper and the Parousia) are not treated.

19. Bornkamm, "Letter to the Romans," 31.

20. Cf. Bornkamm, *Paul,* 88–96, 241–43; Willi Marxsen, *Introduction to the New Testament* (Philadelphia: Fortress Press, 1968), 92–109; Robert Jewett, *A Chronology of Paul's Life* (Philadelphia: Fortress Press, 1979); see his appended chart after p. 160; and Koester, *Introduction to the New Testament,* 2:138–42.

21. Cf. Cranfield, *Romans,* 17–21. For a survey of the history of the early congregations in Rome, see Wolfgang Wiefel, "The Jewish Community in Ancient Rome and the Origins of Roman Christianity," in *The Romans Debate,* ed. Donfried, 100–119; and more recently the essays on Romans by Raymond E. Brown in Raymond E. Brown and John P. Meier, *Antioch and Rome: New Testament Cradles of Catholic Christianity* (New York: Paulist Press, 1983), 92–127. Brown speaks of "a moderately conservative Jewish/ Gentile Christianity at Rome, sympathetic to Jerusalem" (p. 119).

22. Bornkamm, "Letter to the Romans," 25–27; idem, *Paul,* 93–94; Wilckens, *Römer,* 1:47–48; and Koester, *Introduction to the New Testament,* 2:140.

23. Wilckens, *Römer,* 1:49.

2. God's Righteousness in Christ

The phrase "righteousness of God" appears only occasionally in the letters of Paul (Rom. 1:17; 3:5, 21–22; 10:3; 2 Cor. 5:21; Phil. 3:9). But the phrase expresses a theme far more fundamental to Paul's theology than a statistical survey of such passages would indicate. Recent exegetical and theological work has shown that it is pervasive and foundational in Paul's theology, and that it is basic to an understanding of other themes including, for example, justification by faith.

The phrase is easily misunderstood. The word "righteousness" has meanings in English that are for the most part foreign to the biblical meanings. This is also the case with other European languages. For example, the Greek phrase *dikaiosynē theou* ("righteousness of God") was translated by the Latin Fathers and the Vulgate as *iustitia dei* ("justice of God"), which has had a significant impact on exegesis and theology ever since. When the English word "righteousness" is heard, one tends to think of conformity to an absolute ethical norm, and so the phrase "righteousness of God" is heard to signify the standard of righteousness that God requires of persons in the final judgment.

Contemporary discussion of the phrase has centered around certain key issues. Exegetical work has focused sharply on the questions of (1) the syntax of the phrase in Paul's usage and (2) whether there were pre-Pauline models in the Old Testament, Judaism, or early Christianity upon which Paul built. Studies have also dealt vigorously with the question of the role of the phrase in Pauline theology as a whole. The discussion that follows will begin with a review of the debate in exegetical work, and then move on to seek a way through the debate in order to grasp Paul's understanding of the phrase and to see how it plays a major role in his proclamation and theology.

THE SEARCH FOR
MODELS AND MEANING

The specific phrase "righteousness of God" (*dikaiosynē theou*) appears explicitly seven times in the letters of Paul (Rom. 1:17; 3:5, 21, 22; 10:3 twice; and 2 Cor. 5:21). Beyond this, Paul speaks of "his [= God's] righteousness" in two instances (Rom. 3:25, 26), and on one occasion he speaks of "the righteousness from God" (*hē ek theou dikaiosynē*, Phil. 3:9).

Interpreters have disagreed on how the phrase should be interpreted in light of the basic patterns of Greek syntax. The phrase consists of a noun in the nominative case ("righteousness") followed by a noun in the genitive (*theou*, "of God"). The point of disagreement is over the kind of genitive being used in decisive contexts. Interpreters may agree that Paul uses more than one type of genitive in the phrase, depending upon the passage under investigation, but they assert that one usage is dominant in Paul and theologically more significant.

There are two basic interpretations that have been offered in modern times. On the one hand, it is said that Paul makes use of the "genitive of origin" (or *genitivus auctoris*), in which the meaning of the phrase would be that "righteousness" proceeds from God (as its originator, much as a book proceeds from its author) and is bestowed on the believer as an alien righteousness. In this instance Rom. 10:3 and Phil. 3:9 are taken to be decisive for interpreting the concept and all other passages. On the other hand, it is said that Paul makes use of the "subjective genitive," by which the noun in the genitive (God, in this case) is the subject of the action expressed, so that the phrase expresses God's dynamic, saving action toward the world, which has been manifested already in the cross of Christ and is operative still in the gospel. In this instance Rom. 1:16–17 and 3:21–22 are taken as decisive for interpreting the concept and all other passages.[1]

The debate has taken place chiefly in Germany and particularly among the post-Bultmannians and those influenced by them. But the debate has been picked up subsequently in places outside Germany and continues in international scholarship, so that the concept of the "righteousness of God" in Paul is one of the most widely controverted

topics in Pauline studies, and it is so partly because it has major consequences for theology.

In his *Theology of the New Testament* Rudolf Bultmann treated
the "righteousness of God" as the first topic under the larger category
of "Man under Faith."[2] The consequence of his ordering of the discussion was to understand "righteousness" in general and the "righteousness of God" in terms of the standing of the believer before God. By
so doing, Bultmann stood squarely within the legacy of the Reformation. According to this tradition, a person stands before God as a
sinner, but God has made the sinless Christ become sin (2 Cor. 5:21)
and die on the cross for sinful humanity. Those who accept this event
in faith receive an "alien righteousness" from God. Although Bultmann does not say in this particular place that Paul makes use of the
"genitive of origin," that is implied, and he says so forthrightly in a
subsequent essay.[3] In his discussion Bultmann starts out by saying that
for Paul, as for Judaism before him, righteousness is the condition for
receiving salvation. The term *dikaiosynē* can have an "ethical" sense,
but it can also have a "forensic" sense:

> When it denotes the condition for (or the essence of) salvation,
> *dikaiosynē is a forensic term.* It does not mean the ethical quality of
> a person. It does not mean any quality at all, but a relationship. That
> is, *dikaiosynē* is not something a person has on his own; rather it is
> something he has in the verdict of the "forum" (law court — the sense
> of "forum" from which "forensic" as here used is derived) to which he
> is accountable. He has it in the opinion adjudicated to him by another
> . . . but he is "righteous" not to the extent that he may *be* innocent,
> but to the extent that he is *acknowledged* innocent.[4]

Starting from this discussion of righteousness as that which is the
condition (or even precondition) of salvation — starting from the
human side of the relationship — Bultmann does not actually treat the
phrase "righteousness of God" apart from the human condition. For
Paul, he says, *dikaiosynē* is a "forensic-eschatological term."[5] Righteousness is imparted to a person in the present on the basis of faith:

> God already pronounces His eschatological verdict (over the man of
> faith) in the present; the eschatological event is already present reality,
> or, rather, is beginning in the present. Therefore, the righteousness
> which God adjudicates to man (the man of faith) is not "sinlessness"

in the sense of ethical perfection, but is "sinlessness" in the sense that God does not "count" man's sin against him (II Cor. 5:19). . . . When God rightwises the sinner, "makes him righteous" (Rom. 4:5), that man is not merely "regarded as if" he were righteous, but really is righteous — i.e. absolved from his sin by God's verdict.[6]

In this way of understanding the term, the "righteousness of God" is the righteousness that comes from God to the believer. It has its "origin in God's grace"[7] (genitive of origin). The reason that "righteousness" is called "God's righteousness" is that "its one and only foundation is God's grace — it is God-given, God-adjudicated righteousness," and Bultmann points to Rom. 10:3 and Phil. 3:9 as the basis for viewing it as such.[8]

Many interpreters of Paul in the twentieth century have stood in the same camp with Bultmann. Anders Nygren, for example, wrote that the "righteousness of God" is the same as the "righteousness from God" (Phil. 3:9).[9] It is not a "property" of God. Rather, "the righteousness of God is a righteousness which He reveals to us and permits us to share. Hence it is indeed man's righteousness too."[10] It is a "righteousness originating in God, purposed by God, revealed in the gospel and therein offered to us."[11] Bornkamm has written that the term is a "genitive of origin."[12] The relationship of humanity to God is a legal one.[13] God's righteousness is conveyed to believers, for God attributes his righteousness to them, pronouncing them righteous.[14] Likewise, other recent interpreters of Paul — such as Hans Conzelmann, Eduard Lohse, Herman Ridderbos, and C. E. B. Cranfield — have concluded that Paul uses the genitive of origin in the phrase.[15] Conzelmann says forthrightly that the focus of Paul is anthropological.[16] The righteousness of God is an "alien righteousness" bestowed on the believer.[17] Lohse writes that God's righteousness is God's gift to faith.[18] Ridderbos goes so far as to say that the "righteousness of God" is the righteousness bestowed by God upon the believer which is required for the latter to go free in the divine judgment.[19] For Cranfield, Paul makes use of a "genitive of origin," and *dikaiosynē* "refers to man's righteous status which is the result of God's action of justifying."[20]

In 1961 Ernst Käsemann raised the question of the meaning of the Pauline phrase and proposed a radical revision of our understanding of it.[21] Käsemann argued that at certain points (e.g., Rom. 3:5, 25–26) one must understand the phrase as clearly employing the subjective genitive, for it speaks of God's activity or nature.[22] The problem with the genitive of origin is that it emphasizes the individual over against God in such a way that the individual's own righteousness—received as a gift—becomes a kind of personal possession, cut off from the giver, the Lord.[23] Based on a juridical model, the accent is wholly on the individual's status before God (an anthropological interest), rather than upon God's righteousness as a power at work in the world (a theological, or theocentric, concept)—which the subjective genitive implies.

Käsemann argues that the "righteousness of God" concept was not invented by Paul. It appears, after all, elsewhere in the New Testament itself (Matt. 6:33; James 1:20) and can be traced back to the Old Testament (Deut. 33:21) and early Judaism. In the latter instance, he says, one can point to the *Testament of Dan* 6.10 ("Depart, therefore, from all unrighteousness, and cleave unto the righteousness of God"[24]) and the Qumran *Manual of Discipline* ("If I stagger because of the sin of flesh, my justification shall be by the righteousness of God,"[25] 1QS 11.12). In the Old Testament and in Jewish texts that speak of the "righteousness of God" there is no hint of a personal, ethical quality—necessary for one's standing before God—which one receives; rather, a relationship is meant.[26] The formulation speaks of God's saving activity.[27] God's righteousness is God's "power which brings salvation to pass"[28] (German: *heilsetzende Macht*[29]). Furthermore, he says, "the gift which is being bestowed here is never at any time separable from its Giver. It partakes of the character of power, in so far as God himself enters the arena and remains in the arena with it."[30] By this Käsemann means that in Pauline thought God's power takes possession of those under the lordship of Christ so that, in the words of Paul, "it is no longer I who live, but Christ who lives within me" (Gal. 2:20).[31] No one can boast of achievements. "Only so long as we keep on the pilgrim way and allow ourselves to be recalled daily to the allegiance of Christ, can we abide in the gift which we have received and can it abide, living and powerful, in us."[32] In a sentence Käsemann sums up: "*dikaiosynē theou* is for Paul God's sovereignty over the world revealing itself eschatologically in Jesus."[33]

Käsemann's position had been anticipated by Martin Luther's insight that God's righteousness in the Pauline writings is God's power to justify. In his lectures on Romans (1515–16) Luther had written, "God is called righteous by the apostle because he justifies or makes us righteous."[34] But Luther himself did not carry out the consequences of his insight consistently. In some instances he understood the phrase "righteousness of God" to signify that righteousness which counts before God, given by God himself, in the act of justifying the believer, while in other places (chiefly after 1545) he spoke of God's righteousness as God's salvation-creating, justifying action.[35] There are instances in the works of John Calvin at which he approaches Luther's insight, particularly in his *Institutes*, in which God's righteousness is linked with "the divine promise" (3.18.7) and "God's mercy" (3.11.18), but neither Calvin nor Philip Melanchthon interpreted Pauline texts along these lines in their commentaries.[36] Later Protestant orthodoxy—in developing the doctrine of justification by faith—understood the "righteousness of God" as that righteousness which is necessary for humankind in the final judgment, and which is granted to the believer.[37]

In modern times Käsemann's position was anticipated by other interpreters, even if not fully achieved. Already in the nineteenth century Herman Cremer had indicated that the term "righteousness of God" is a "relational concept" rather than an objective standard.[38] Shortly after the turn of the century James H. Ropes had indicated that the term had a soteriological connotation in light of its Old Testament background.[39] Charles H. Dodd in his commentary (1932) had written concerning the term at Rom. 1:17 that here Paul speaks of "a divine activity" which "is taking place manifestly within the field of human experience."[40] Adolf Schlatter wrote in a book published in 1935 that the expression speaks of a "relationship" created between God and humanity and that its essential meaning is God's "saving power" (*rettende Kraft*).[41] Gottlob Schrenk had asserted that Paul uses the subjective genitive.[42] And Albrecht Oepke had written that the phrase is a technical term used already in the Old Testament and in Judaism prior to Paul, and that Paul's usage must be analyzed in terms of this background.[43]

Subsequent to his essay, Käsemann's position has been influential and a basis for several longer studies.[44] Books have appeared that draw upon his insights and seek to show that the "righteousness of God" in Paul refers to the saving activity of God rather than to God's standard of judgment or to the righteousness required of humanity before God. These are books by Christian Müller,[45] Peter Stuhlmacher,[46] Karl Kertelge,[47] J. A. Zeisler (with qualifications),[48] and John Reumann.[49] Käsemann's influence can also be seen in the treatments of Paul's theology in works of Werner G. Kümmel,[50] Victor P. Furnish,[51] Ulrich Wilckens,[52] J. Christiaan Beker,[53] and Leonhard Goppelt.[54] On the other hand, Bultmann wrote an article in direct response to Käsemann's essay, rejecting his position and reaffirming his own earlier position.[55] Conzelmann, Lohse, Ridderbos, and Cranfield have likewise (in the works already referred to in our previous discussion) responded directly to Käsemann's essay, reaffirming the view that Paul makes use of a "genitive of origin" and that his interest is anthropological, that is, that the "righteousness of God" is a righteousness bestowed on the believer.[56]

OBSERVATIONS ON THE SEARCH

The debate over the meaning of the phrase "righteousness of God" continues. Decisions on the matter are influenced by various perspectives brought by the interpreter. Nevertheless, there are some things that can be said, based on the data.

1. Interpreters frequently point to Deut. 33:21 as containing a phrase that provides the Hebrew equivalent to — and model for — the Greek *dikaiosynē theou*.[57] No other Old Testament texts can be cited in addition as offering an equivalent. But it must be noted that even in the case of this passage, the Hebrew does not actually speak of the "righteousness of God" but of the "righteousness of the Lord," which would be the equivalent of *hē dikaiosynē tou kyriou* (or *dikaiosynē kyriou*) in Greek. In Deuteronomy 33 Moses blesses the tribes of Israel. In his blessing of the tribe of Gad, he recounts that Gad had "executed the righteousness of the Lord (*ṣidqat Yahweh*) and his judgments with Israel" (33:21). The LXX alters the verse considerably, having "the Lord" as subject of the clause: "The Lord executed his righteousness (*dikaiosynēn kyrios epoiēsen*) and judgment with Israel." It is highly dubious then whether Deut. 33:21 can be considered a model or background for the Pauline phrase. The Hebrew text speaks of the "righteousness of the Lord," and regardless of how one

judges the significance of this as background for the concept, at least it can be said that the LXX does not provide a model for Paul's phrase (in its entirety). Moreover, neither Philo nor Josephus makes use of the phrase.[58] Philo lists righteousness (*dikaiosynē*) among the attributes of God—his "wisdom, understanding, and righteousness" (*Deus Imm.* 79)—and in one instance he writes of God as the one who guarantees to demonstrate in judgment "truth and righteousness" (*Vit. Mos.* 2.237–38). Likewise, Josephus speaks of God's righteousness (*dikaiosynē*), but only on one occasion (*Ant.* 11.267), and in that instance it refers to an attribute of God along with his wisdom.

2. The closely related phrase *dikaiosynē [tou] kyriou* appears only twice in the LXX. In 1 Sam. 12:7 (LXX, 1 Kingdoms) Samuel is speaking to all Israel and says, "I shall declare to you every *dikaiosynēn kyriou*, those things which he did among you and your fathers." Here, however, the phrase means "every saving deed of the Lord." At Mic. 6:5 the prophet speaks for the Lord, recounting the Lord's saving deeds "in order that *hē dikaiosynē tou kyriou* might be known." Again, the phrase means the "saving deed of the Lord." Aside from these two instances, the term "righteousness" is linked with God or the Lord at two other places, in which "righteousness" (rather than God or the divine name) is set in the genitive case, attributing righteousness to God (in the manner of an adjective). The question is raised in Mal. 2:17, "Where is the God of righteousness (*ho theos tēs dikaiosynēs*)?" And at Tob. 13:7 there is the exhortation, "Bless the Lord of righteousness (*ton kyrion tēs dikaiosynēs*)." The phrase "righteousness of God" (*dikaiosynē theou*), however, is lacking in the LXX.

3. Nevertheless, the entire phrase *dikaiosynē theou* does exist in Hellenistic sources outside the writings of Paul. It appears in the *Testament of Dan* 6.10 ("Depart, therefore, from all unrighteousness, and cleave unto the righteousness of God, and your race will be saved for ever"[59]). Whether this passage is to be considered to be from the hand of a Jewish or a Christian writer is virtually impossible to judge,[60] but it is a clear instance of the use of the phrase. The phrase also appears at James 1:20 and 2 Pet. 1:1 (and echoes of it appear at Matt. 6:33). These sources document the existence of the phrase in Jewish and/or Jewish Christian Hellenistic tradition, but four observations should be made: (1) such evidence is meager; (2) the passages

offer no further clues concerning the origins of the phrase, since Paul antedates James, 2 Peter, and Matthew, and he may well antedate the *Testament of Dan* as well; (3) the meaning of the phrase in James 1:20 is actually quite different from Paul's;[61] and (4) while the meaning of the phrase in 2 Pet. 1:1 may be similar to Paul's, it does not attest to the circulation of a common technical term in early Christianity, for the author is acquainted with the apostle's writings (cf. 3:15–16) and writes presumably well into the second century.

4. Although the entire phrase "righteousness of God" is not found in the Old Testament, the concept exists frequently in instances that speak of "his [= God's] righteousness," "your [= God's] righteousness," etc. Concerning such usage, Gerhard von Rad has written that two concepts are excluded from the term: (1) that it refers to an absolute norm, established by God, by which humanity is measured; and (2) that it carries a punitive meaning.[62] On the contrary, the term refers to God's saving acts in history, and it can be a synonym for salvation.[63] This can be confirmed by reference to many texts, and it is seen especially clearly in cases of parallelism, such as in Ps. 98:2 (LXX, 97:2):

> The Lord has made known his salvation (*sōtērion*);
>   before the nations he has revealed his righteousness (*dikaiosynēn*).

Other instances of the parallelism are found at Ps. 40:10 (LXX, 39:11); 51:14 (LXX, 50:16); Isa. 46:13; 51:5–6; 61:10 (Hebrew only); and 62:1.

5. The term "righteousness of God" appears in Hebrew at Qumran. It appears explicitly in the *Manual of Discipline* (or *Rule Scroll*):

> If I stagger because of the sin of flesh,
> my justification (*mišpāṭi*) shall be
> by the righteousness of God (*beṣidqat 'ēl*)
> which endures for ever. (1QS 11.12)[64]

The term also appears explicitly in the same scroll at 10.25–26 and in the *War Scroll* (1QM 4.6). In several other instances God's "righteousness" is referred to—without the full phrase, but as "his" or "your" (= God in both cases) righteousness—as well.[65] It is clear then that the "righteousness of God" was an idiom or theological term in

Judaism at the dawn of the Christian era, even if it cannot be documented unequivocally in Hellenistic texts prior to the writings of Paul. Furthermore, it should be observed that in the sectarian literature of Qumran one does not find the term found at Deut. 33:21, the "righteousness of Yahweh." The Qumran community generally avoided the use of the divine name,[66] and so the term "righteousness of God" was used instead.[67]

THE BACKGROUND FOR
PAUL'S CONCEPT IN SCRIPTURE
AND TRADITION

It can be seen from the foregoing that the term "righteousness of God" cannot be shown to have been a phrase familiar to Paul from the LXX or Hellenistic Judaism, of which he was a spiritual heir. At least it can be said that the phrase is not current in the literary sources we possess. Whether it was current in oral traditions or in the piety of the synagogue we do not know, although that is unlikely in light of the sources we have. The Qumran texts attest to its usage in Hebrew, but again we are left in the dark concerning the question whether the phrase had currency in the theological or cultic traditions with which Paul had been familiar.

Some interpreters have concluded that the phrase existed in the pre-Pauline Christian tradition. Conzelmann and Lohse, for example, point to Rom. 3:25–26 as evidence, claiming that here Paul made use of a pre-Pauline formula.[68] Yet it cannot be established for certain that these verses constitute a pre-Pauline tradition; in fact, as will be shown in the next chapter, these verses can be considered a Pauline composition, even if he made use of traditional terms. Another passage—which contains the phrase "righteousness of God"—sometimes cited as pre-Pauline is 2 Cor. 5:21.[69] Does this provide evidence for a pre-Pauline origin of the term? Again, it is held by other interpreters that this verse is a Pauline (rather than pre-Pauline) composition.[70] Stuhlmacher, for instance, emphasizes that the verse speaks of "sin" in the singular, which is typical of Paul, whereas pre-Pauline traditions tend to speak of "sins" (cf. 1 Cor. 15:3–4).[71]

What can be seen clearly is that the term "righteousness of God" appears in passages that are undisputedly Pauline compositions elsewhere (Rom. 1:17; 3:5, 21; 10:3; Phil. 3:9). It is not clear that the term belonged to the "living language" of the church prior to Paul. Possibly it did, but this cannot be documented for certain.[72] What is certain is that Paul made use of the phrase; that he was one of the first — perhaps the very first — to do so in early Christianity; and that, in any case, it was for him a vital theological concept.

But from where would Paul have derived the concept, or on what basis would he have coined the phrase, if indeed that is what happened? As indicated previously, he would not have derived it from Deut. 33:21. But he could have coined the phrase from his acquaintance with Old Testament texts, mediated through Greek translation, which speak of the revelation of God's righteousness as an eschatological act, and particularly those texts that speak of an expected messianic figure (hereafter "the Messiah") as manifesting the righteousness of God. Most of these texts are found in the Psalms, Isaiah, and Jeremiah. They are texts that Paul would have confronted in searching the Scriptures in light of the cross and resurrection of Jesus as the Christ. For Paul, the death of Christ was the means by which God acted decisively for the salvation of the human race. The act of God in sending his Son was the supreme moment of the manifestation of his righteousness (Rom. 3:21–22), and the gospel is itself the means by which the righteousness of God is revealed (Rom. 1:17).

There are several passages in the LXX (from which the following quotations are translated) that speak of the "righteousness" that would be manifested with the coming of the Messiah:

> Behold, the days are coming, says the Lord, and I shall raise up
>   for David a righteous scion (*anatolēn dikaian*),
> And as a king he shall reign and understand and do justice
>   and righteousness (*dikaiosynēn*) upon the earth.
> In his days Judah will be saved, and Israel will dwell securely.
> And this is the name which will be given to him,
>   Lord of righteousness (*kyrios Iōsedek*).
>
> (Jer. 23:5–6)

> Give, O God, your judgment to your king
>   and your righteousness (*dikaiosynēn*) to the king's son
> to judge your people in righteousness (*dikaiosynē*)
>   and your poor in judgment.

Let the mountains bear peace for your people,
  the hills also, in righteousness (*dikaiosynē*).
He shall judge the poor of the people
  and he shall save the sons of the needy. . . .
In his days righteousness (*dikaiosynē*) shall spring up,
  and an abundance of peace, until the moon is taken away.
                          (Ps. 72:1–4, 7; LXX, 71:1–4, 7)

His rule shall be great,
  and of his peace there is no end
  upon the throne of David and his kingdom
  to establish it and to uphold it
  in righteousness (*dikaiosynē*) and in judgment
  from now and for ever.
                          (Isa. 9:7; LXX, 9:6)

And then shall come forth a shoot from the stump of Jesse
  and a branch shall rise up from the stump.
And the spirit of God shall rest upon him. . . .
And he shall be girded about his loins with righteousness (*dikaiosynē*)
  and his sides with truth.
                          (Isa. 11:1–2, 5)

For [the Lord] comes to judge the earth;
  he will judge the world with righteousness (*dikaiosynē*)
  and peoples with his truth.
                          (Ps. 96:13; LXX, 95:13)

And for you who fear my name
  the sun of righteousness (*dikaiosynēs*) shall rise
  and healing in his wings;
and you shall go out and leap as calves released from bonds.
                          (Mal. 4:2; LXX, 3:20)

And the Lord wills to remove the travail of his soul
  to show him light and to fashion [him] with understanding
  to vindicate the righteousness one (*dikaion*) in his service of many,
  and he will bear their sins.
                          (Isa. 53:10b–11)

Another passage that speaks of the righteousness of the Messiah is Jer. 33:14–16, but this passage is not given in the LXX.

Still other passages in the LXX speak of the revelation of God's righteousness echatologically, which Paul would have understood as having been confirmed in the coming of the Messiah:

Truth has sprung up from the earth
  and righteousness (*dikaiosynē*) has stooped down from heaven.
For the Lord will grant goodness
  and our earth will give its fruit;
Righteousness (*dikaiosynē*) will go before him,
  and he will prepare a way for his steps.

(Ps. 85:11–13; LXX, 84:12–14)

The Lord has made known his salvation (*sotērion*);
  before the nations (*ethnē*) he has revealed (*apokalypsen*)
  his righteousness (*dikaiosynēn*). . . .
For he comes to judge the earth;
  he will judge the world in righteousness (*dikaiosynē*)
  and the peoples with uprightness.

(Ps. 98:2, 9; LXX, 97:2, 9)

Let heaven rejoice from above
  and the clouds sprinkle righteousness (*dikaiosynēn*).
Let the earth bring forth mercy
  and let it bring forth righteousness (*dikaiosynēn*)
  at the same time.

(Isa. 45:8)

Turn to me and be saved,
  those who are from the end of the earth.
I am God, and there is no other.
By myself I swear,
  Truly righteousness (*dikaiosynē*) shall go forth from my mouth;
  my words shall not return.
For every knee shall bow to me,
  and every tongue shall confess to God, saying,
Righteousness (*dikaiosynē*) and glory shall come to him,
  and all who separate themselves shall be put to shame.
From the Lord they shall be justified (*dikaiōthēsontai*),
  and in God they shall be glorified,
  every offspring of the sons of Israel.

(Isa. 45:22–25)

My righteousness (*dikaiosynē*) approaches quickly,
  and my salvation (*sotērion*) shall go forth as the light,
  and the nations (*ethnē*) shall hope in my arm. . . .
And my salvation (*sotērion*) will be forever,
  and my righteousness (*dikaiosynē*) shall not cease.

(Isa. 51:5–6)

For the sake of Zion I shall not be silent,
  and for the sake of Jerusalem I shall not rest
  until my righteousness (*dikaiosynē*) goes forth as light
  and my salvation (*sōtērion*) burns as a torch.
And nations (*ethnē*) shall see your righteousness (*dikaiosynēn*)
  and kings your glory.

(Isa. 61:1-2)

And as the earth brings forth its flower
  and as a garden [brings forth] its seeds,
so the Lord will cause righteousness (*dikaiosynēn*)
  and gladness to spring up before all the nations (*ethnē*).

(Isa. 61:11)

Beyond the Old Testament, there are other passages and traditions in intertestamental and later Jewish literature that speak of righteousness in connection with the Messiah or messianic age. In the *Psalms of Solomon*, which derive from Pharisaic circles of the second half of the first century B.C.[73] — and as Pharisaic stand in the same tradition as Paul did — there are several references to the Messiah and his righteousness. It is said that "God will make him . . . wise . . . with strength and righteousness" (17.42 [37]); he will "lead in righteousness" a holy people (17.28 [26]); he will "judge peoples and nations in the wisdom of his righteousness" (17.31 [29]); and he will be "a righteous king" (17.35 [32]).[74] In the Similitudes of Enoch (chapters 37–71 of *Ethiopian Enoch*) — which are thought by some to contain traditions that antedate the rise of Christian literature[75] — it is said concerning the Son of man that he is "born unto righteousness, and righteousness abides over him, and the righteousness of the Head of Days forsakes him not" (71.14).[76] Moreover, "He proclaims . . . peace in the name of the world to come" and "righteousness never forsaketh him" (71.15).[77] The messianic figure is called the "Righteous One" (38.2; 53.6). "Righteousness shall prevail in his days, and the righteous and elect shall be without number before Him for ever and ever" and "righteousness before him shall never fail" (39.6–7).[78] Again, "This is the Son of Man who hath righteousness, with whom dwelleth righteousness, and who revealeth all the treasures of that which is hidden" (46.3).[79] Still other passages on the manifestation of righteousness in the messianic age are found in the Wisd. of Sol. 5:18 and Bar. 5:9.

Other sources, both Jewish and Christian, of later points in time, also attest to the righteousness of the Messiah. The *Testament of Judah* does so in 24.1–6. The text may be a Christian composition (interpolation), so it is difficult (perhaps impossible) to know whether it reflects Jewish or Christian messianism (or both).[80] Nevertheless, it conveys a tradition that links righteousness with the Messiah in antiquity. In this passage it is said that "a star shall arise" from Jacob (Israel) "like the sun of righteousness, walking with the sons of men in meekness and righteousness." "He shall pour out the spirit of grace upon you." From him "shall grow a rod of righteousness to the Gentiles, to judge and to save all that call upon the name of the Lord" (24.1, 3, 6).[81]

The Messiah is also a figure endowed with or acting through "righteousness" in various traditions in the New Testament (Matt. 3:15; Acts 17:31; Heb. 1:9; 7:2–3; 1 John 2:28–29; 3:7; 2 Pet. 1:1; Rev. 19:11; cf. also 2 Pet. 3:13), including of course the writings of Paul (Rom. 5:18; 1 Cor. 1:30). At other places in the New Testament the Messiah Jesus is called "righteous" (John 5:30; 1 Pet. 3:18; 1 John 2:1, 29; 3:7; Rev. 15:3; cf. Luke 23:47; 1 John 1:9).

Later Jewish traditions continue to speak of the Messiah as righteous. In the rabbinic, midrashic *Pesikta Rabbati* 37.2 it is said, "And when the Messiah appears, He will be clothed in righteousness, as is said, 'And he put on righteousness as a coat of mail' (Isa. 59:17)."[82] In the *Midrash on Psalms* the Messiah is designated as bearing righteousness (21.2; 72.5).[83] The term "Messiah of righteousness" is found in the Targum on Jeremiah (23.6).[84] Sigmund Mowinckel has offered still further references in the rabbinic material and summarizes by saying that the Messiah's righteousness implies his just government and judgment of his people, but "as a rule" the term is "closely associated with salvation. . . . The righteousness of the Messiah consists in his saving his people: righteousness and salvation are identical."[85]

THE PAULINE SYNTHESIS

The debate over the meaning of "the righteousness of God" in Paul, as indicated in "The Search for Models and Meaning" and "Observations on the Search" above, has centered largely on (1) the syntax of the phrase and (2) appeals to models in the Old Testament and Jewish literature. Yet the meaning must finally be resolved in light of other considerations, particularly Paul's own usage.[86]

It can be shown (see "Pauline Contexts" below) that, in fact, Paul makes use of both the "genitive of origin" and the "subjective genitive" in speaking of the "righteousness of God." It is not a matter of either/or, but both/and. Moreover, the discussion should take into consideration still other passages in Paul that reflect the background of the term in Scripture and tradition (as illustrated in "The Background for Paul's Concept in Scripture and Tradition").

Among the texts cited above from the LXX, there is only one that appears to have been alluded to directly by Paul. At Rom. 1:17 Paul says that the righteousness (*dikaiosynē*) of God has been revealed (*apokalyptetai*), which appears to be an allusion to Ps. 98:2 (LXX, 97:2): "Before the nations [God] has revealed (*apokalypsen*) his righteousness (*dikaiosynēn*)." At Rom. 3:21 it appears that a similar allusion is made. Paul also quotes from Isa. 45:23 among the passages presented above ("Every knee shall bow to me, and every tongue confess to God") — with slight variations — at Rom. 14:11 and in the pre-Pauline Philippian Hymn (2:10–11), but the lines that speak of God's "righteousness" are not quoted. One cannot maintain therefore that all (or even most) of the passages cited above formed specific scriptural bases for Paul's use of the "righteousness of God" formulation. On the other hand, neither can such passages be ignored. In the seven letters undisputedly written by Paul, he makes (according to one listing) some seventy-seven direct quotations from the Old Testament. Out of these seventy-seven there are sixteen (20.8 percent) from the Psalms and twenty-three (29.9 percent) from Isaiah.[87] When allusions are added to the totals, Paul (according to another listing) has some 187 quotations and allusions in the same letters. Out of these 187, there are thirty-five (18.7 percent) from the Psalms and forty-six (24.6 percent) from Isaiah.[88] Paul would then have been familiar with texts and Jewish traditions that speak of the coming of the righteousness of God with the Messiah or messianic age. In fact this is indicated by his statement in Rom. 3:21 that the "law and the prophets" (=Hebrew Scriptures) attest to the righteousness of God, which has *now* been made manifest in the advent of the crucified, resurrected Messiah.

Here it is fruitful to bring other texts into the discussion. At 1 Cor.

1:30 Paul writes concerning Christ that he is the one

> who was made wisdom for us by God,
> [our] righteousness (*dikaiosynē*), sanctification, and redemption.

Here, using the divine passive ("was made"), Paul asserts that God has made Christ Jesus our wisdom, righteousness, sanctification, and redemption. Paul speaks elsewhere of Christ as the "wisdom of God" (1 Cor. 1:24) and as the one whose death is a means of redemption (Rom. 3:24) and sanctification (1 Cor. 6:11). For Paul the promises of the manifestation of God's righteousness with the coming of the Messiah or in the messianic age — a tradition that endures in the literature of Judaism and elsewhere in the New Testament — have been confirmed in the atoning death of Jesus, whom God has made our righteousness. This motif appears also at Rom. 5:18 where Paul writes that, in antithesis to the condemnation that has come upon all from Adam's transgression, "one man's act of righteousness (*dikaiōma*) leads to justification (*dikaiōsin*) resulting in life for all persons."[89] Jesus, whose death is atoning, is the one who bears righteousness/justification into the world, because he is the Messiah of righteousness. In him the promise of the manifestation of God's righteousness with the coming of the Messiah or in the messianic age has been confirmed.

A similar motif comes to expression in Rom. 10:3-4. Here Paul contrasts Israel's attempt to establish righteousness by works of the law, which has been a failure, with the righteousness of God. Then he goes on to say that Christ is the "end (*telos*) of the law." Exegetes differ over the meaning of *telos* in this context. Some see it as meaning merely "purpose" (so Christ is the fulfillment of the law's true meaning).[90] But that is to stop short of the radicality of the Pauline gospel. For Paul, Christ in the "end" of the law as a means of salvation (cf. Rom. 3:20; 8:3; Gal. 2:16, 21; 3:10, 21),[91] and the Christian is no longer under law but under grace (Rom. 6:14; cf. Gal. 5:18).[92] To put it another way, Christ replaces the law. He is the "end of the law for righteousness to everyone who believes" (Rom. 10:4b). The nuance can be missed easily. Christ is said to be not only the "end of the law" but "for righteousness" (*eis dikaiosynēn*) to everyone who believes. The law as a means of righteousness has ended, and in its place Christ stands "for righteousness," that is, the Messiah who brings God's righteousness into the world. As the law had been God's revelation to Israel and the means of establishing righteousness for salvation (cf. Lev. 18:5), now Christ is God's revelation and means of establishing righteousness for salvation. Through the crucified Christ, God has manifested his righteousness once and for all; the Messiah brings righteousness into the world, as promised. No one can establish righteousness by the law (Rom. 3:20). One is justified (right-wised) through faith in the Messiah who is himself the expression of the righteousness of God. Faith is the acceptance of the righteousness of God which has come into the world through Christ.

Before leaving this discussion of the righteousness that is personified, or even incarnated, in the Messiah, it should be noted that 1 Cor. 1:24 and 30 express a "wisdom Christology."[93] Behind such a Christology lies a complex history which cannot be reviewed here. Suffice it to say that as early as Deut. 4:6 there is an association of wisdom and the law: "keep [God's statutes and ordinances] and do them; for that will be your wisdom." And the identification of wisdom and Torah is made explicit in Sir. 24:3–9, 23 (cf. also Bar. 3:9 – 4:4). Furthermore, wisdom and righteousness are identified in Jewish traditions prior to the time of Paul (Prov. 8:8, 15–16, 20; Wisd. of Sol. 8:7; 9:3; Sir. 45:26). So wisdom is said to declare, "I walk in the ways of righteousness" (Prov. 8:20). For Paul, Christ replaces the Torah (Rom. 10:4), and both the wisdom of God (1 Cor. 1:24, 30) and the righteousness of God (Rom. 10:3–4; 1 Cor. 1:30) are incarnated in him.

In light of this discussion, it is not necessary, nor finally helpful, to make an exclusive choice between the two dominating interpretations of the "righteousness of God" concept in Paul.[94] The crucified Christ, whose death is atoning, bears "righteousness from God" into the world, which the Old Testament and Jewish traditions held as promise concerning the Messiah. In this sense those who argue for a "genitive of origin" are correct. Christ has been made (by God) "righteousness" for us (1 Cor. 1:30). On the other hand, it is in the crucified Christ, whose death is atoning, that the "righteousness of God" has been manifested *now* (Rom. 3:21, 26) in the messianic age which has dawned upon the world. In this sense those who contend for a "subjective genitive" are also correct. Matters of syntax and the search for a technical term in the Old Testament and later Jewish literature as a model are insufficient to arbitrate the matter, for the Christocentric gospel of Paul is rooted in the promises of God and Jewish expectations concerning the Messiah's coming—the one who is righteousness by divine appointment, who brings righteousness, and whose atoning death is the manifestation of the righteousness of God toward the world.

PAULINE CONTEXTS

It is conceded by various interpreters that at Rom. 3:5 ("But if our wickedness serves to show the righteousness of God, what shall we say?") Paul makes use of the subjective genitive, contrasting human wickedness and divine righteousness.[95] Passages under dispute are Rom. 1:17; 3:21–26 and, to some extent, 10:3. At Rom. 1:17 Paul writes that "in [the gospel] the righteousness of God is revealed through faith for faith; as it is written, 'He who through faith is righteous shall live.'" Bultmann has written that in this instance the phrase "righteousness of God" designates not the action (of God) as such, but its consequence (*Ergebnis*),[96] whereas for Käsemann Paul is speaking here of an earthly epiphany of the righteousness of God.[97] Interpreters thus deliberate as to where the accent should fall. Is the accent of Paul on the revelation of righteousness "for faith" and its consequent effect of justifying the believer who receives it (Bultmann), or is the accent to be placed on the act of revelation itself (Käsemann)?

Every term and phrase of Rom. 1:16–17 is important. In 1:16 Paul has written that the gospel is "the power of God unto salvation to everyone who believes, to the Jew first and also to the Greek." Then in 1:17 he goes on to say that in the gospel the righteousness of God is revealed. The point to observe is that in this context it is the gospel to which Paul gives attention; it is the subject of the first sentence, and it is the occasion and basis for his speaking of the righteousness of God in the second. The gospel concerning God's Son is revelatory, revealing the "righteousness of God . . . from faith (*ek pisteōs*) to faith (*eis pistin*)," that is, God's righteousness is perceived by faith as having been revealed in the gospel, and it is directed toward faith which receives it.[98] Therefore Paul goes on to quote from Hab. 2:4 (although not rendering it exactly in the form given in the Hebrew text or the LXX), affirming that the one who is righteous by faith (*ek pisteōs*) "shall live," meaning that this person shall have life in the new age which has come and endures eternally. But where in all this does the accent lie? Does Paul accent the theological or the anthropological side of righteousness? There can be little doubt that the accent lies on the former, without excluding the latter. Within the broader context Paul refers to the gospel of God's Son (1:3), a gospel that he serves (1:9), that he is eager to proclaim at Rome (1:15), and of which he is not ashamed, for it is the power of God for salvation to all who believe (1:16). In this very gospel the righteousness of God is revealed (1:17). Apart from the gospel, received by faith, there is no revelation of God's righteousness, for it is only in the gospel of the Messiah, received by faith, that the righteousness of God is beheld. And the promise of the prophet that "the one who is righteous by faith shall live" is now confirmed. The promise is confirmed because the attendant promise that God's righteousness would be made manifest in the coming of the Messiah has been fulfilled in the death of Jesus as the Messiah, which is an atoning death for humankind.

At Rom. 1:17 therefore the phrase "righteousness of God" must be understood as an instance in which the subjective genitive is employed. The gospel refers to a historical event — the crucifixion of the Messiah — that took place in time and space. The gospel refers to that event, but it is more than a historical report. The gospel is itself a power (*dynamis*) from God for salvation. That is so because it overthrows the way of salvation that requires righteousness by the law, and it sets salvation on another foundation altogether. When Paul speaks of the righteousness of God in this instance, and says that it is revealed in the gospel, he does not speak primarily of a righteousness that is imputed to the believer. He is speaking of a righteousness revealed in the gospel of God's Son, the saving message of how God has sent his Son for the salvation of sinful humanity. God's righteousness is God's saving activity which is spoken of in the Scriptures of Israel and promised with the coming of the Messiah or the messianic age.

The same usage (with the subjective genitive) appears at Rom.

3:21–22. In Rom. 3:9–20 Paul establishes that all humankind is under the power of sin. He calls forth the Scriptures of Israel to witness that, in spite of claims to righteousness under the law, the Scriptures themselves attest that no one is righteous. The passages cited in this section are from the Psalms and Isaiah (Pss. 14:1–2; 53:1–2; 5:9; 140:3; 10:7; Isa. 59:7–8; Ps. 36:1). In a rather surprising choice of terminology, however, he speaks of all these citations as from "the law" (3:19), that is, the Hebrew Scriptures in their entirety. And he concludes that "no human being will be justified by works of the law, since through the law comes knowledge of sin" (3:20).

"But *now*," he says, "apart from the law the righteousness of God has been manifested" (3:21). The righteousness of God has been manifested in God's action toward the world in the sending of his Son, whose death is atoning (3:25). Yet even this action is attested in the Scriptures of Israel ("the law and the prophets," 3:21b). Here Paul connects the *now* of the manifestation of God's righteousness with those passages of Scripture that promise the manifestation of God's righteousness at the coming of the Messiah or the messianic age. He does not cite specific promises in the Scriptures here any more than he does in the creedal formula of 1 Cor. 15:3–4. He simply alludes to the witness (*martyroumenē*) of the Scriptures that God's righteousness is to be made manifest with the coming of the Messiah, and he claims that "now" that eschatological promise has been fulfilled. The promised manifestation of righteousness is made evident "through faith in Jesus Christ to all who believe" (3:22).[99] Only through the epistemology of faith is it evident, a faith that sees that God has acted for the salvation of the world through the death of the Messiah Jesus. The atoning death of the Messiah Jesus is a "demonstration of [God's] righteousness" (3:25–26) "in the present time" (3:26a), showing that God is "righteous" and "justifies the person who has faith in Jesus" (3:26b).[100] The entire paragraph (3:21–26) is theocentric and speaks of God's "right-wising" activity in the present (3:21, 26) as a consequence of sending his Messiah to atone for sin, bearing the righteousness of God into the world with saving effect, and therefore making it possible for the one who has faith to receive justification apart from the law.

At Rom. 10:3 the issue of whether Paul uses the subjective genitive or the genitive of origin is less clear. In this context Paul speaks of

Israel. He writes that the people of Israel "have a zeal for God, but not according to knowledge" (or recognition of the truth, 10:2). "For being ignorant of the righteousness of God, and seeking to establish their own, they did not submit to the righteousness of God" (10:3). Bultmann has written that here Paul speaks of the righteousness of God as a gift bestowed.[101] And Cranfield says that in this context the "righteousness of God" means "the status of righteousness which is given by God, since it is opposed to . . . a status of righteousness achieved by their own efforts."[102] Yet it must also be observed that in this context epistemological terminology abounds.[103] For Paul, Israel lacks knowledge and is ignorant of the righteousness of God, which has streamed forth in the crucifixion of the Messiah and is proclaimed in the gospel. It is in consequence of unbelief and lack of the "knowing" that comes from faith that Israel persists in seeking to establish righteousness by the law for salvation. The obedience of faith, on the other hand, perceives that God has acted toward the world, fulfilling his promises that with the Messiah his righteousness shall be made manifest. Zeal for God, apart from the epistemology of faith, leads to seeking one's own righteousness through the law (cf. 9:22, 31). But the righteousness from God overturns this way of seeking righteousness for salvation. The righteousness of God, now made manifest (1:17; 3:21–26), is not simply a gift bestowed, but a saving action in fulfillment of the promises of God, perceived by faith. Christ is the end of the law "for righteousness (*eis dikaiosynēn*) to everyone who believes" (10:4). That is, to faith—a new way of knowing, which comes through the proclamation of the gospel of Christ (10:17)— Christ has replaced the law. He is the decisive revelation of God (as the Torah had been), and he brings forth into the world the righteousness of God, which is apprehended by faith. The NEB translates the verse well: "Christ ends the law and brings righteousness for everyone who has faith."

There are other instances, however, in which the forensic and gift-character of righteousness appear, and in these instances the genitive of origin is employed. The prime example is Phil. 3:9 where Paul writes that he has set aside the righteousness that he had claimed prior to his apostleship under the law (3:8), "in order that I might be found in him, not having my own righteousness from the law, but through faith in Christ the righteousness from God (*ek theou*) on the basis of faith" (3:9). Here Paul sets in contrast righteousness under the law and righteousness "from God" through faith.[104] Furthermore, at Rom. 5:17 Paul speaks of the "free gift of righteousness" for those who receive it, and which has come through Christ. Finally, at 2 Cor. 5:21 Paul writes that for our sake God made his Son to be sin, who knew no sin, "in order that we might become the righteousness of God in him." In each of these instances the anthropological, rather than the theological, accent is present, but even here the Pauline emphasis is solely upon the righteousness of God as that which comes to believers in confirmation of his promises concerning the coming of righteousness through the Messiah. As Abraham believed the promises of God, and it was reckoned to him as righteousness (Gen. 15:6; Rom. 4:3; Gal. 3:6), so all are justified (accounted righteous) through faith in the Messiah, whose atoning death is a confirmation of the divine promise that in Abraham all the nations will be blessed (Gen. 13:3), for in the atoning death of Jesus as the Messiah, the blessing has extended to the gentiles (Gal. 3:14). God bestows upon the believer his righteousness as a gift (Rom. 5:17); righteousness comes from God through faith (Phil. 3:9); and in Christ's death an interchange takes place in which he assumes sin, and believers become "the righteousness of God" (2 Cor. 5:21), which can be taken as a virtual equivalent of "being justified."[105]

The yield of such a survey shows that both the subjective genitive and the genitive of origin conceptions appear in Paul. The former accents the divine action; the latter accents consequent justification by faith, by which believers receive God's gift of righteousness by faith. But in both cases, Christ's atoning death is the middle term, for it both manifests God's righteousness and bears God's righteousness into the world. This leads to the topic of justification, which is to be pursued later (in chapter 4). But the question must first be pursued as to how the two ways of speaking are related.

PAUL AND THE GOSPEL
OF THE RIGHTEOUSNESS OF GOD

The exegetical and theological tradition since the Reformation has tended to stress the forensic and gift-character of righteousness. The anthropological interest has predominated. This approach arises out of the question of how one stands before God, and the resolution of the question has been worked out with the concept of an "alien righteousness" which is granted to the believer by God.

That this approach and accent was made during the Reformation and in its wake can be understood in light of the theological and pastoral needs of the time. And consequent developments can also be understood. Early Protestantism had to build a theological system based on Scripture, and the Reformation principle of justification by faith as the one article of faith by which the church stands or falls had to be worked into the dogmatic system. But the method and legacy of early Protestant theology was to produce primarily a *system* supported by reference to biblical texts,[106] and the method tended to blot out certain themes within Scripture in favor of bringing selected texts to the fore in order to give a "biblical" basis for the *loci* (or topics) of dogmatics. The Pauline theme concerning the righteousness of God is one such theme that was blotted out.

When the term "righteousness" appears in the works of early Protestant dogmatics, it is coupled with the righteousness of Christ or the righteousness that the believer has (or must have) before God. References to the "righteousness of God" are almost lacking. When the phrase does appear, it is equated with God's holiness and wrath. In the *Formula of Concord* (within the Lutheran confessional writings), for example, it is said that Paul refers to the hardening of Pharaoh's heart (Rom. 9:17–18) as an example "for the sole purpose of thereby setting forth the righteousness of God which God manifests toward the impenitent and despisers of his Word."[107] And Calvin in his *Institutes* (2.7.6) speaks of God's righteousness as being revealed in the law, which convicts and condemns. Otherwise the term "righteousness" appears in connection with justification within early Protestant theological writings, and it is understood in a forensic way. This is the case in both Lutheran and Reformed traditions. Within the Lutheran tradition, the *Apology to the Augsburg Confession* states this clearly: "'To be justified' here does not mean that a wicked man is made righteous but that he is pronounced righteous in a forensic way."[108] Or again (in reference to Rom. 5:1) the same document says: "In this passage 'justify' is used in a judicial way to mean 'to absolve a guilty man and pronounce him righteous,' and to do so on account of someone else's righteousness, namely, Christ's, which is communicated to us through faith."[109] J. A. Quenstedt (1617–88) — sometimes called the "bookkeeper of orthodoxy"— wrote that the Greek and Hebrew terms for justification speak of God's "justifying the wicked before His tribunal," and therefore these terms "have a forensic signification."[110] The righteousness of Christ is imputed to the believer, as Quenstedt expresses it: "Our justification before God consists in the remission and non-imputation of sins and the imputation of the righteousness of Christ."[111] Again, the *Formula of Concord* states: "God forgives us our sins purely by his grace . . . and reckons to us the righteousness of Christ's obedience, on account of which righteousness we are accepted by God into grace and are regarded as righteous."[112] Likewise, Calvin has many passages in his *Institutes* that speak of the righteousness of Christ as a gift bestowed to the believer. He writes, for example, that "we are justified before God solely by the intercession of Christ's righteousness. This is equivalent to saying that man is not righteous in himself but because the righteousness of Christ is communicated to him by imputation" (3.11.23).[113]

It is clear that the early dogmatic writers of the Reformation era had rediscovered the essentials of justification in the Pauline writings and elaborated the concept well for their own times. But their writings and legacy within Protestantism have tended to place front and center the model of the law court and judicial proceedings, and that is a narrowing of the Pauline gospel. The picture portrayed is that of a God seated on the judge's bench, and before whom each individual is a guilty sinner. The sinner needs to be justified before him in order to go free in the final judgment. But God is a merciful judge, and so he pronounces the sinner righteous (i.e., justifies) on the basis of the righteousness of Christ, the sinless one, which is imputed to the one who will accept it. This way of thinking has persisted not only in Protestant theology but in interpretations of Paul to the present day. It appears, for example, when Ridderbos speaks of the "righteousness of God" as "righteousness that can stand before God" and "what man requires in order to go free in the judgment."[114]

It must be granted that there are passages in which Paul speaks in terms of (or at least implies) a righteousness before God as necessary for justification (Rom. 2:13; Gal. 2:16; cf. Rom. 3:20), so the forensic model is not lacking. But Paul transcends this model, as can be seen in the following points.

1. As indicated earlier (chapter 1), at the basis of Paul's theology is not a doctrine but an event, the appearance of the crucified and resurrected Christ to him. The pre-Pauline gospel that Jesus is the Christ, who was crucified for us in an atoning death, was certified to him in the appearance of this crucified and resurrected one. It is precisely the old model — in which one has to appear before God as justified (by works of the law) to go free in the judgment — that is overturned. The old model is no longer operative. In its place is not a new model, but rather the promise of God in the Scriptures of Israel — particularly in the Psalms and the prophets — that God would manifest his righteousness with the coming of the Messiah or messianic age. In the atoning death of Christ the righteousness of God has been revealed (Rom. 1:17; 3:21), and the gospel is therefore the power of God for salvation, for it attests to the saving work of God apart from the law.

2. The forensic (anthropological/anthropocentric) imagery is all but completely overshadowed by apocalyptic (theological/theocentric) imagery.[115] While a forensic residue remains (and that will be explored in chapter 4 under "Justification by Faith"), Paul's gospel essentially sets forth a message of the *revelation* of God's righteousness. The forensic model is anthropological and anthropocentric: how can the sinner be justified before God? The apocalyptic imagery employed by Paul is theological and theocentric: what does the gospel of the atoning death of Christ say about God and God's action toward the world?

3. The gospel of the righteousness of God is the basis for the doctrine of justification by faith apart from the law.[116] The distinction of terminology used here is significant. Gospel and doctrine are different kinds of discourse. Gospel is good news addressed to the hearer in the act of proclamation. Paul speaks of the gospel as the "gospel of God" (Rom. 1:3; 15:16; 2 Cor. 11:7; 1 Thess. 2:2, 8, 9), the "gospel of his Son" (Rom. 1:9), and most often the "gospel of Christ" (Rom. 15:19; 1 Cor. 9:12; 2 Cor. 2:12; 9:13; 10:14; Gal. 1:7; Phil. 1:27; 3:2). It is in the gospel that the righteousness of God is revealed (Rom. 1:17). The gospel bears the good news of God's saving activity, his

righteousness, for the fallen world, delivering humankind from the powers of the present evil age (Gal. 1:4). The promise of God to reveal his righteousness in the coming of the Messiah or messianic age has been confirmed in the atoning death of Christ, who was "put to death for our trespasses and raised for our justification" (Rom. 4:25) — God being the actor (as the passive verbs attest concerning Christ). It is on the basis of this gospel of the righteousness of God in Christ that the doctrine of justification is constructed. If it is the case — as it is — that God has acted decisively for the salvation of humanity in Christ, then it follows doctrinally that justification comes not from the doing of works of the law, but through accepting that in Christ God has done what the law could not do (Rom. 8:3; cf. 10:3–4; Phil. 3:9).

4. The consequences of the Pauline gospel of the righteousness of God are far-reaching theologically. It is on the basis of this gospel that Paul had a theological outlook that transcended an individualistic interpretation of the scope of grace in Christ. He was able to say that the scope of grace in Christ reaches out toward all humanity (Rom. 5:12–21) and indeed to the redemption of the whole creation (Rom. 8:18–25). During the course of ongoing history, the gospel is for all humanity; there is no distinction between Jew and gentile (Rom. 3:29; Gal. 3:28). The church is the community of the redeemed on earth, upon whom the end of the ages has already come (1 Cor. 10:11). The church is the nucleus of all the "nations" to be redeemed; it is this nucleus that by faith has apprehended the righteousness of God and testifies to it in the world. Yet the scope of the redemptive work of God in Christ is finally more inclusive than the circle of believers, and it will be certified at the Parousia "when all things are subjected" to Christ, and then to God the Father, and God is "everything to everyone" (1 Cor. 15:28). This strain of thinking is made even more explicit in the deutero-Pauline letter to the Colossians, by which an early interpreter of Paul wrote concerning Christ that "all things were created through him and for him" (1:16), and that "in him all the fulness of God was pleased to dwell, and through him to reconcile to himself all things, whether on earth or in heaven, making peace by the blood of the cross" (1:19–20). This theme of the relationship between the reconciliation or justification of all human-

ity and the particularity of justification by faith will be developed further in chapter 4.

5. The theological legacy of the church, especially since the era of orthodox Protestantism, has stressed the justification of the individual. It has been taught, in line with Paul, that justification is not by works of the law, but through faith. But there are recurring tendencies within theology and proclamation to make faith into another form of work, which the individual must exercise in order to appropriate the righteousness of God offered in Christ. Nygren has summarized illustrations from various interpreters who follow such thinking:

> "Faith is the indispensable and only condition for salvation" (Althaus). "Faith is declared to be the only and unfailingly effective condition for the attainment of salvation" (Jülicher). "Faith is the condition on the part of man without which the gospel cannot have power for him" (B. Weiss). "Nothing but faith is demanded in order that man may experience the righteousness of God" (von Hofmann). "The gospel is operative for salvation to every one that has faith; effective without exception for all men under the condition of faith." "Here it needs only to be said that beside the conditions daily fulfilled independently of man, when the gospel is preached, the faith of him who hears is also an inescapable condition" (Zahn). E. Kühl speaks with like intent about "the Achievement of Faith" as the condition on the part of man for justification. And O. Moe affirms what Paul is saying that "there is no other demand but faith." In other words, the issue is "the sufficiency of faith for salvation."[117]

Nygren goes on to say that such interpretations are entirely foreign to Paul's thinking, and in this his judgment is manifestly correct. The flaw in such thinking is that the "righteousness of God" is thought to be solely a righteousness bestowed on the believer, and the flaw is compounded by making faith a precondition (and in a sense a work) for receiving it. But the Pauline gospel is quite different. As Nygren has put it, "faith is evidence that the gospel *has* exercised its power" on the believer. "It is not [one's] faith that gives the gospel its power; quite the contrary, it is the power of the gospel that makes it possible for one to believe."[118] The Pauline gospel reveals the righteousness of God as God's action toward the world, and it is only on the basis of this revelation gospelled into the world that one can believe, trust, and be reconciled to God. This is made clear in the declaration and call of Paul: "In Christ God was reconciling the world to himself"— a bold declaration, an indicative— and on the basis of that follows the call, "We beseech you on behalf of Christ, be reconciled to God" (2 Cor. 5:19–21). That is to say, the good news is that God has already reconciled the world to himself in Christ; for God has made Christ to be sin (2 Cor. 5:21) and has thereby overcome human sin through his own right-wising action. What remains then is the call to humankind to accept the reconciliation that has been given its foundation in the atoning death of Christ. This theme will be developed more fully in the chapters on justification and Paul's apostleship. But first we shall examine a pivotal text which proclaims the gospel of God's righteousness in the atoning death of Christ, by which God has set forth the crucified Christ for the sake of the world.

NOTES

1. It is possible to make even finer distinctions so as to speak of (1) objective genitive, (2) subjective genitive, and (3) genitive of origin. The first, however, is not proposed in current discussions. For a survey of the three senses, see Ulrich Wilckens, *Der Brief an die Römer*, EKKNT 6 (Köln: Benzinger; Neukirchen-Vluyn: Neukirchener, 1978–1982), 1:203; and John Reumann, *"Righteousness" in the New Testament: "Justification" in the United States Lutheran-Roman Catholic Dialogue*, with responses by Joseph A. Fitzmyer and Jerome D. Quinn (Philadelphia: Fortress Press, 1982), 66.

2. Rudolf Bultmann, *Theology of the New Testament* (New York: Charles Scribner's Sons, 1951–55), 1:270–87.

3. Rudolf Bultmann, *"Dikaiosynē Theou," JBL* 83 (1964):12–16.

4. Bultmann, *Theology of the New Testament*, 1:271–72; emphases appear in the English text.

5. Ibid., 1:273.

6. Ibid., 1:276.

7. Ibid., 1:284.

8. Ibid., 1:285.

9. Anders Nygren, *Commentary on Romans* (Philadelphia: Fortress Press, 1949), 75.

10. Ibid., 75.

11. Ibid., 76.

12. Günther Bornkamm, *Paul* (New York: Harper & Row, 1971), 138.

13. Ibid.

14. Ibid., 136–38.

15. Hans Conzelmann, *An Outline of the Theology of the New Testament* (New York: Harper & Row, 1969), 218, and idem, "Paul's Doctrine of Justification: Theology or Anthropology?" in *Theology of the Liberating Word*, ed. Frederick Herzog (Nashville: Abingdon Press, 1971), 108–23 (trans. from the German original which appeared in *EvT* 28 [1968]:389–404); Eduard Lohse, "Die Gerechtigkeit Gottes in der paulinischen Theologie," in *Die Einheit des Neuen Testaments* (Göttingen: Vandenhoeck & Ruprecht, 1973), 223; idem, *Grundriss der neutestamentlichen Theologie* (Stuttgart: Kohlhammer, 1974), 86; Herman Ridderbos, *Paul: An Outline of His Theology* (Grand Rapids: Wm. B. Eerdmans, 1975), 163; C. E. B. Cranfield, *A Critical and Exegetical Commentary on the Epistle to the Romans*, ICC (Edinburgh: T. & T. Clark, 1975–1979), 824–26.

16. Conzelmann, *Outline of the Theology of the New Testament*, 219; idem, "Paul's Doctrine of Justification," especially pp. 119–20.

17. Conzelmann, *Outline of the Theology of the New Testament*, 220.

18. Lohse, *Grundriss*, 86.

19. Ridderbos, *Paul*, 163.

20. C. E. B. Cranfield, *Romans*, 97; cf. 825.

21. Ernst Käsemann, "Gottesgerechtigkeit bei Paulus," *ZTK* 58 (1961): 367–78; reprinted in *Exegetische Versuche und Besinnungen*, 2d ed. (Göttingen: Vandenhoeck & Ruprecht, 1960–1965), 2:181–93. An English version appears as "'The Righteousness of God' in Paul," in *New Testament Questions of Today* (Philadelphia: Fortress Press; London: SCM, 1969), 168–82. References are to the latter, unless specified otherwise. Cf. also Ernst Käsemann, *Commentary on Romans* (Grand Rapids: Wm. B. Eerdmans, 1980), 21–32.

22. Käsemann, "'The Righteousness of God' in Paul," 169.

23. Ibid., 177.

24. Quoted from *APOT* 2:335.

25. Quoted from *The Dead Sea Scrolls in English*, trans. G. Vermes (Baltimore: Penguin Books, 1962), 93.

26. Käsemann, "'The Righteousness of God' in Paul," 172.

27. Ibid., 172, 174.

28. Ibid., 181.

29. Käsemann, "Gottesgerechtigkeit bei Paulus," in *Exegetische Versuche*, 2:193.

30. Käsemann, "'The Righteousness of God' in Paul," 174.

31. Ibid., 173.

32. Ibid., 175.

33. Ibid., 180.

34. Martin Luther, "Lectures on Romans," *Luther's Works* (St. Louis: Concordia Pub. House; Philadelphia: Fortress Press, 1955–76), 25:249.

35. For a survey on Luther, see Peter Stuhlmacher, *Gerechtigkeit Gottes bei Paulus*, FRLANT 87 (Göttingen: Vandenhoeck & Ruprecht, 1965), 19–23.

36. Ibid., 23–25.

37. Texts are cited subsequently in "Paul and the Gospel of the Righteousness of God."

38. Hermann Cremer, *Biblico-Theological Lexicon of New Testament Greek*, 3d ed. (Edinburgh: T. & T. Clark, 1886), 193; idem, *Die paulinische Rechtfertigungslehre im Zusammenhang ihrer geschichtlichen Voraussetzungen*, 2d ed. (Gütersloh: G. Bertelsmann, 1900), 33–34.

39. James Hardy Ropes, "Righteousness in the Old Testament and in St. Paul," *JBL* 22 (1903):211–27.

40. Charles H. Dodd, *The Epistle of Paul to the Romans*, MNTC (New York: Harper & Brothers, 1932), 10.

41. Adolf Schlatter, *Gottes Gerechtigkeit: Ein Kommentar zum Römerbrief*, 2d ed. (Stuttgart: Calwer, 1952), 36, 38. The first edition of this work was published in 1935.

42. Gottlob Schrenk, "*Dikaiosynē* in Paul," *TDNT*, 2:203. The German edition appeared in 1935.

43. A. Oepke, "*Dikaiosynē theou* bei Paulus in neuer Beleuchtung," *TLZ* 78 (1953):257–63.

44. On this, there is an excellent survey by Manfred T. Brauch, "Perspectives on 'God's Righteousness' in recent German discussion," contained as an appendix in E. P. Sanders, *Paul and Palestinian Judaism: A Comparison of Patterns of Religion* (Philadelphia: Fortress Press, 1977), 523–42.

45. Christian Müller, *Gottes Gerechtigkeit und Gottes Volk: Eine Untersuchung zu Römer 9–11*, FRLANT 86 (Göttingen: Vandenhoeck & Ruprecht, 1964).

46. Stuhlmacher, *Gerechtigkeit*.

47. Karl Kertelge, "*Rechtfertigung*" *bei Paulus*, NTAbh, Neue Folge 3 (Münster: Aschendorf, 1967).

48. J. A. Zeisler, *The Meaning of Righteousness in Paul: A Linguistic and Theological Enquiry*, SNTSMS 20 (Cambridge: Cambridge Univ. Press, 1972), 168–71, 186–89, 191.

49. Reumann, "*Righteousness*" *in the New Testament*, 41–123, 187–89.

50. Werner G. Kümmel, *The Theology of the New Testament* (Nashville: Abingdon Press, 1973), 196–98.

51. Victor Paul Furnish, *Theology and Ethics in Paul* (Nashville: Abingdon Press, 1968), 143–46.

52. Wilckens, *Römer*, 1:202–33, et passim.

53. J. Christiaan Beker, *Paul the Apostle: The Triumph of God in Life and Thought* (Philadelphia: Fortress Press, 1980), 262–64.

54. Leonhard Goppelt, *Theology of the New Testament* (Grand Rapids: Wm. B. Eerdmans, 1981–82), 2:140–41.

55. Bultmann, *"Dikaiosynē Theou,"* 12–16. This essay appeared in 1964; see n. 3.

56. See the works cited previously in n. 15.

57. Cf. Käsemann, "'The Righteousness of God' in Paul," 172; and Stuhlmacher, *Gerechtigkeit,* 140.

58. G. Schrenk, *"Dikaiosynē,"* in *TDNT,* 2:193–94; Stuhlmacher, *Gerechtigkeit,* 142–45.

59. Quoted from *APOT,* 2:335.

60. For a discussion of the provenance and authorship of the *Testaments of the Twelve Patriarchs,* see Leonhard Rost, *Judaism Outside the Hebrew Canon: An Introduction to the Documents* (Nashville: Abingdon Press, 1976), 140–44; and George W. E. Nickelsburg, *Jewish Literature between the Bible and the Mishnah* (Philadelphia: Fortress Press, 1981), 231–34.

61. Cf. Zeisler, *The Meaning of Righteousness,* 135, who writes that it refers to the righteousness God demands, not to God's own saving righteousness.

62. Gerhard von Rad, *Old Testament Theology* (New York: Harper & Row, 1962–65), 1:370–71, 377. Cf. also Elizabeth R. Achtemeier, "Righteousness in the Old Testament," *IDB,* 4:80–85; and Klaus Koch, *"Sdq,"* in *Theologisches Handwörterbuch zum Alten Testament,* ed. E. Jenni and C. Westermann (Munich: Chr. Kaiser, 1971–1972), 2:517–18.

63. von Rad, *Old Testament Theology,* 1:372, 377.

64. Quoted from *The Dead Sea Scrolls in English,* trans. G. Vermes, 93; the Hebrew is supplied from *Die Texte aus Qumran,* ed. Eduard Lohse (Munich: Kösel, 1964), 40.

65. See Helmer Ringgren, *The Faith of Qumran* (Philadelphia: Fortress Press, 1963), 63–67.

66. Ibid., 47–48. Cf. also the survey of Qumran texts by George Howard, "The Tetragram and the New Testament," *JBL* 96 (1977):65–72.

67. Stuhlmacher, *Gerechtigkeit,* 154.

68. Conzelmann, *An Outline of the Theology of the New Testament,* 219; Lohse, *Einheit,* 220; idem, *Grundriss,* 85–86.

69. Ernst Käsemann, "Some Thoughts on the Theme, 'The Doctrine of Reconciliation in the New Testament,'" in *The Future of Our Religious Past,* ed. James M. Robinson (New York: Harper & Row, 1971), 52–55; and Reumann, *"Righteousness" in the New Testament,* 33–35.

70. Stuhlmacher, *Gerechtigkeit,* 74–77; and Wilhelm Thüsing, "Rechtfertigungsgedanke und Christologie in den Korintherbriefen," in *Neues Testament und Kirchen,* ed. J. Gnilka (Freiburg: Herder, 1974), 310–11. Zeisler, *The Meaning of Righteousness,* 159–61, assumes it to be Pauline.

71. Stuhlmacher, *Gerechtigkeit,* 74–75.

72. This does not mean, however, that the concept of justification cannot be found prior to Paul. That it is pre-Pauline is shown by Reumann, *"Righteousness" in the New Testament,* 27–40, in regard to various creedal

statements.

73. Cf. Rost, *Judaism Outside the Hebrew Canon*, 119; Nickelsburg, *Jewish Literature*, 203–4.

74. Quoted from *APOT*, 2:649–50.

75. Cf. Rost, *Judaism Outside the Hebrew Canon*, 138–39; G. Nickelsburg, *Jewish Literature*, 221–23.

76. Quoted from *APOT*, 2:237.

77. Quoted from ibid.

78. Quoted from ibid., 2:210–11.

79. Quoted from ibid., 2:214.

80. On the complicated history of the text of the *Testaments of the Twelve Patriarchs*, see Rost, *Judaism Outside the Hebrew Canon*, 140–46; and Nickelsburg, *Jewish Literature*, 231–34.

81. Quoted from *APOT*, 2:323–24.

82. Quoted from *Pesikta Rabbati*, trans. William G. Braude (New Haven, Conn.: Yale Univ. Press, 1968), 2:689.

83. *The Midrash on Psalms*, trans. William G. Braude (New Haven, Conn.: Yale Univ. Press, 1959), 1:294, 562.

84. Cf. Marcus Jastrow, *A Dictionary of the Targumim, the Talmud Babli and Yerushalmi, and the Midrashic Literature* (New York: Pardes, 1950), 2:1263.

85. Sigmund Mowinckel, *He That Cometh* (Nashville: Abingdon Press, 1954), 308–9.

86. Cf. Conzelmann, *Outline of the Theology of the New Testament*, 218.

87. This data is based on the lists provided by Henry B. Swete, *An Introduction to the Old Testament in Greek*, rev. Richard R. Ottley (Cambridge: Cambridge Univ. Press, 1914; reprint, New York: KTAV, 1968), 389–90.

88. This data is based on the lists provided by Brooke F. Westcott and Fenton J. Hort, *The New Testament in the Original Greek* (New York: Macmillan Co., 1953), 608–11.

89. The translation "justification resulting in life" is taken from Cranfield, *Romans*, 269.

90. Ibid., 515–20; George Howard, "Christ the End of the Law: The Meaning of Romans 10:4ff.," *JBL* 88 (1969):331–37; Paul Meyer, "Romans 10:4 and the End of the Law," in *The Divine Helmsman: Studies on God's Control of Human Events*, ed. J. L. Crenshaw and S. Sandmel (New York: KTAV, 1980), 68; W. S. Campbell, "Christ the End of the Law: Romans 10:4," in *Studia Biblica 1978: III. Papers on Paul and Other New Testament Authors*, ed. E. A. Livingstone, JSNTSup 3 (Sheffield: JSOT Press, 1980), 73–81; and C. Thomas Rhyne, *Faith Establishes the Law*, SBLDS 55 (Chico, Calif.: Scholars Press, 1981), 95–116.

91. William Sanday and Arthur C. Headlam, *A Critical and Exegetical Commentary on the Epistle to the Romans*, 5th ed., ICC (Edinburgh: T. & T. Clark, 1902), 284–85; Bultmann, *Theology of the New Testament*,

1:263; Nygren, *Romans*, 379–80; C. K. Barrett, *A Commentary on the Epistle to the Romans*, HNTC (New York: Harper & Brothers, 1957), 197–98; Käsemann, *Romans*, 280–83; Morna D. Hooker, *A Preface to Paul* (New York: Oxford Univ. Press, 1980), 29; Sam K. Williams, "The 'Righteousness of God' in Romans," *JBL* 99 (1980):284; Heikki Räisänen, "Paul's Theological Difficulties with the Law," in *Studia Biblica 1978*, ed. E. A. Livingstone, 306; Wilckens, *Römer*, 2:221–24; idem, "Statements on the Development of Paul's View of the Law," in *Paul and Paulinism: Essays in Honour of C. K. Barrett*, ed. M. D. Hooker and S. G. Wilson (London: SPCK, 1982), 17–18; S. Kim, *The Origins of Paul's Gospel*, WUNT 2/4 (Tübingen: J. C. B. Mohr [Paul Siebeck], 1981), 308; and E. P. Sanders, *Paul, the Law, and the Jewish People* (Philadelphia: Fortress Press, 1983), 38–41. A similar view is expressed ("the way of the Law gives place to the law or way of Christ") by W. D. Davies, "Paul and the Law: Reflections on Pitfalls in Interpretation," in *Paul and Paulinism*, ed. M. D. Hooker and S. G. Wilson, 10.

92. Of course if Christ is the terminus of the law, that does not preclude, but indeed includes his fulfillment of its purpose; the latter interpretation alone, however, precludes the former, and that is its limitation.

93. On wisdom Christology in Paul, see especially W. D. Davies, *Paul and Rabbinic Judaism: Some Rabbinic Elements in Pauline Theology*, 4th ed. (Philadelphia: Fortress Press, 1980), 147–76. On wisdom traditions as background for New Testament Christology, see Reginald H. Fuller, *The Foundations of New Testament Christology* (New York: Charles Scribner's Sons, 1965), 72–75; and Reginald H. Fuller and Pheme Perkins, *Who Is This Christ?* (Philadelphia: Fortress Press, 1983), 53–66.

94. Cf. the same judgment in Roy A. Harrisville, *Romans*, ACNT (Minneapolis: Augsburg Pub. House, 1980), 33.

95. Cf. Bultmann, "*Dikaiosynē Theou*," 13; Cranfield, *Romans*, 96; Conzelmann, *Outline of the Theology of the New Testament*, 218; Käsemann, "'The Righteousness of God' in Paul," 169; Stuhlmacher, *Gerechtigkeit*, 84–86; Kertelge, "*Rechtfertigung*," 67; Zeisler, *The Meaning of Righteousness*, 170; and Richard B. Hayes, "Psalm 143 and the Logic of Romans 3," *JBL* 99 (1980):111. Although the term "subjective genitive" is not used, it is implied in the discussion of David R. Hall, "Romans 3.1–8 Reconsidered," *NTS* 29 (1983):188–90.

96. Bultmann, "*Dikaiosynē Theou*," 14.

97. Käsemann, "'The Righteousness of God' in Paul," 173; cf. idem, *Romans*, 30. See also D. H. van Daalen, "The Revelation of God's Righteousness in Romans 1:17," *Studia Biblica 1978*, ed. E. A. Livingstone, 383–89.

98. Cf. Käsemann, *Romans*, 30–31; Harrisville, *Romans*, 26, 30; and Williams, "The 'Righteousness of God' in Romans," 256.

99. On the expression "faith of Jesus Christ" (Paul's expression) in Rom. 3:22, 26, and elsewhere as meaning "faith in Jesus Christ," see Arland J. Hultgren, "The *Pistis Christou* Formulation in Paul," *NovT* 22 (1980):248–63.

100. Cf. Werner G. Kümmel, "*Paresis* and *Endeixis*: A Contribution to the Understanding of the Pauline Doctrine of Justification," in *Journal for Theology and the Church 3*, ed. R. W. Funk (New York: Harper & Row, 1967), 1–13.

101. Bultmann, "*Dikaiosyne Theou*," 13.

102. Cranfield, *Romans*, 97.

103. On the "epistemology of faith" in another context, see J. Louis Martyn, "Epistemology at the Turn of the Ages: 2 Corinthians 5:16," in *Christian History and Interpretation: Studies Presented to John Knox*, ed. W. R. Farmer, C. F. D. Moule, and R. R. Niebuhr (Cambridge: Cambridge Univ. Press, 1967), 269–87.

104. Cf. Wilckens, *Römer*, 1:206–7.

105. So Cranfield, *Romans*, 97–98; Wilckens, *Römer*, 1:207.

106. Cf. Gerhard Ebeling, "The Meaning of 'Biblical Theology,'" in *Word and Faith* (Philadelphia: Fortress Press, 1963), 79–97.

107. *Formula of Concord*, SD 11.86; quoted from *The Book of Concord*, ed. Theodore G. Tappert (Philadelphia: Fortress Press, 1959), 631.

108. *Apology* 4.252; quoted from ibid., 143. Cf. also *Apology* 4.72 (p. 117).

109. *Apology* 4.305; quoted from ibid., 154.

110. Quoted from Heinrich Schmid, *The Doctrinal Theology of the Evangelical Lutheran Church*, 3d ed. (reprint, Minneapolis: Augsburg Pub. House, 1961), 427.

111. Ibid., 429.

112. *Formula of Concord*, Ep. 3.4; quoted from *Book of Concord*, 473.

113. Quoted from John Calvin, *Institutes of the Christian Religion*, ed. John T. McNeill, LCC (Philadelphia: Westminster Press, 1960), 1:753.

114. Ridderbos, *Paul*, 163.

115. Cf. Wilckens, *Römer*, 1:221.

116. Cf. Ibid., 1:208.

117. Nygren, *Romans*, 68.

118. Ibid., 71.

3. God's Act in Christ

Among the various passages in Paul's letters that speak of the atoning death of Christ, and that also speak of this event in connection with the manifestation of the righteousness of God and consequent justification, Rom. 3:21–26 stands out supreme.[1] It has been suggested that the section contains pre-Pauline traditions and liturgical phrases.[2] Nevertheless, it has been composed in its present form by the apostle himself, and it contains his gospel in miniature. The passage poses some difficulties for the interpreter, however, and it is our purpose here to confront those difficulties and to seek to interpret this passage and related passages to discern the Pauline doctrine of the atoning death of Christ.

THE CRUCIFIED CHRIST AND CULTIC IMAGERY

One of the most disputed passages in the interpretation of Paul's letters is Rom. 3:25, in which Paul writes of Christ as the one "whom God put forth as an *hilastērion*." What is the meaning of the Greek term *hilastērion*? The term has been translated in various ways, as follows:

Vulgate (fifth century): *propitiationem* (propitiation)
Luther's German New Testament (1522): *Gnadenstuhl* (mercy seat)
Tyndale (1534): "seate of mercy"
KJV (1611): "propitiation"
ASRV (1901): "propitiation"
RSV (1946): "expiation"
NEB (1961): "means of expiating sin"

JB (1966): using a circumlocution, "to sacrifice his life so as to win
   reconciliation"

TEV (1966): "means by which men's sins are forgiven"

NAB (1970): "means of expiation"

NIV (1973): "a sacrifice of atonement"

The history of exegesis is likewise varied. What follows is a review
of this history and an evaluation of various positions taken. The section following this review seeks to make a proposal concerning this
oft-disputed passage.

Early Christian writers interpreted the passage by making use of
"typological" exegesis, that is, that method that discerns events or
institutions in the Old Testament as foreshadowing or prefiguring
events or meanings in reference to Christ and his saving work. Old
Testament events or institutions are "types," "prototypes," or illustrations of what is to be fulfilled in Christ, and the latter events or
meanings are the "antitypes."[3]

In the case of Rom. 3:25, the term *hilastērion* is seen in typological
exegesis to have been derived from certain texts in the LXX. In
Exodus 25, Moses is given directions by God to build furnishings for
the tabernacle. In Exod. 25:10–22 various specifications for the ark of
the covenant are given. Among them, Moses is to make a *kappōreth*
(RSV, "mercy seat"), which is translated in the LXX as *hilastērion
epithēma* at Exod. 25:17, but elsewhere simply as *to hilastērion*
(Exod. 25:18–22; 31:7; 35:12; 38:5, 7–8 [Hebrew: 37:6–9]; Lev. 16:2,
13–15; Num. 7:89). The *kappōreth* was to be made of pure gold and
in the shape of a flat slab (two and one-half cubits long; one and one-
half cubits wide) with two golden cherubim—one on each end. It
was placed over the ark itself (Exod. 25:21), and it was considered to
be the place at which the Lord would meet the priestly representa-
tives of the people (25:22).[4] It was to be located in the "most holy
place" of the tabernacle (26:34). Later, after the construction of the
Jerusalem Temple, the ark of the covenant (with the *kappōreth*) was
placed in the "most holy place" (or "holy of holies") of the Temple (1
Kings 8:6; 2 Chron. 5:7).

The typological significance of the *kappōreth/hilastērion* centers in
its function within the cultus of Israel on the Day of Atonement, as
prescribed in Leviticus 16. On this day the high priest must enter into

the holy of holies to make atonement for sins. Among his duties is that of sprinkling blood from a slain bull on the front of the *kappōreth* and seven times before it (16:14). Then he is to sprinkle the blood of a slain goat upon and before it (16:15). These rites, together with the sin offerings (16:11, 15), are performed to make expiation for the priest himself (16:6, 11, 17, 24), the community (16:10, 17, 24), and for the holy place itself (16:20).[5]

If typology has been employed at Rom. 3:25, this will mean that for Paul (and/or perhaps a tradition before him) the crucified Christ is the "antitype" for which the Old Testament *kappōreth* serves as the "type." The "mercy seat" instituted by God (Exodus 25) as the place where atonement is made (Leviticus 16) prefigures the death of Christ, which is then the once-for-all divine act of atonement.

Whether that was Paul's meaning or not, that was how Rom. 3:25 was interpreted by various early Christian writers. Origen (ca. A.D. 182–251), whose commentary on Romans has survived in a Latin translation from an earlier Greek version, claimed that the background of Rom. 3:25 is to be found in the Old Testament account of God's directing Moses to make a *propitiatorium*, which is related at Exod. 25:10–22. The term *propitiatorium* means "propitiatory" or "place of propitiation" and is the term used in Latin versions of the Old Testament, including the Vulgate, to translate *kappōreth* (LXX, *hilastērion*). The *propitiatorium* of the Old Testament cultus is called by Origen a *figura* ("figure" or "type," the term used in typolological correlations within Latin texts) of what was to come, and by implication Christ is then the "antitype."[6]

Besides Origen, other interpreters saw a typological correlation as well. Eusebius of Caesarea (A.D. 260–339) wrote concerning Rom. 3:25 that the whole human race was in need of a "living and true expiation, of which the *hilastērion* constructed by Moses produced a type (*typos*), and this was our Savior and Lord, the Lamb of God."[7] Theodoret (ca. A.D. 393–466) wrote concerning Rom. 3:25 that "the true mercy seat (*hilastērion*) . . . is Christ. For he fulfills the old as a type (*typos*)."[8] And John of Damascus (ca. A.D. 700–753), when commenting on Rom. 3:25, wrote, "See how [Paul] recalls things in the Old [Testament]; . . . there was, as the type (*typos*), the *hilastērion*."[9]

The Vulgate breaks rank with the typological correlation. In the

Old Testament *kappōreth/hilastērion* is rendered as *propitiatorium* ("propitiatory" or "place of propitiation") at Exod. 25:17–22; 31:7; 35:12; 37:6–9; Lev. 16:2, 14–15; Num. 7:89. The same term is used at Heb. 9:5. But at Rom. 3:25 *hilastērion* is translated as *propitiationem* ("propitiation"). Here the typological correlation has given way to the view that Christ is the one "whom God put forth as a propitiation . . . for a display of his justice" (*quem proposuit Deus propitiationem per fidem in sanguine ipsius ad ostensionem iustitiae suae*).[10]

During the Reformation era the typological interpretation was revived. Martin Luther's lectures on Romans (1515–16), as preserved, do not yet go in this direction. But in his translation of the New Testament (1522) Luther translated the term *hilastērion* at both Rom. 3:25 and Heb. 9:5 as *Gnadenstuhl* ("mercy seat"). In his later translation of the entire Bible (1534) Luther continued this usage and used the same term in the Old Testament passages (Exodus, Leviticus, and Numbers). It is regretted that we have no explanation for Luther's decision (e.g., whether he had knowledge of the church fathers at this point, or whether he rediscovered the linguistic and typological connections himself), but it is clear that he perceived the typological correlation and translated accordingly.[11] Likewise, John Calvin, in his commentary on Romans (1539), allows the possibility of typology here in Paul: "There seems to be an allusion in the word *hilastērion* . . . to the ancient propitiatory; for he teaches us that the same thing was really exhibited in Christ, which had been previously typified."[12] Yet Calvin does not finally decide the issue, for he allows that appeasement of the Father may be the meaning (by implication then Christ would be the "propitiation"). Finally, William Tyndale, who resided in Germany and became acquainted with Luther, translated *hilastērion* as "seate of grace" at Rom. 3:25 in his English translation of the New Testament in 1525. In his translation of the Old Testament (1530) he rendered *kappōreth* as "merci seate." And in his revised translation of the New Testament (1534) he rendered *hilastērion* at Rom. 3:25 as "seate of mercy."[13] But the translators of the KJV (1611) did not follow Tyndale. While the term "mercy seat" was used for the Old Testament passages and at Heb. 9:5, the term "propitiation" was used at Rom. 3:25. This is what had been provided in the Vulgate earlier. In both instances it must be seen that a break has been made so that the imagery is no longer that of a "place" of atonement but is rather that of its "victim."

In modern times translators and exegetes have not agreed on the meaning of *hilastērion* at Rom. 3:25. In the nineteenth century the term was taken to have a typological meaning, corresponding to the Old Testament *kappōreth*, in the studies of Albrecht Ritschl,[14] E. H. Gifford,[15] Hermann Cremer,[16] and J. A. Bengel.[17] On the other hand, there was also at this time a decisive shift from that view in the works of Bernhard Weiss,[18] Adolf Deissmann,[19] and in the commentary of William Sanday and Arthur C. Headlam,[20] the first edition of which appeared in 1895. In each instance (despite variations in approach) the conclusion was that *hilastērion* should not be understood to signify the Old Testament *kappōreth*, but "means of propitiation" (Weiss), "propitiatory gift" (Deissmann), or "propitiatory sacrifice" (Sanday-Headlam).

In the twentieth century, research and debate have gone forth, but still no consensus has been achieved. A new approach was pioneered by Charles H. Dodd. But the result was not to arbitrate between "mercy seat" and "propitiation" — deciding which is to be preferred — but to add a third possibility: "expiation," "means of expiation," or "expiatory sacrifice."[21] Each of the three possibilities (mercy seat, propitiation, and expiation) has arguments in its favor. We cannot review the sequence of debate — for that would be too extensive — but can only cite the basic arguments for each position.

Since the late nineteenth century, there has been a more extensive search into the background of the term *hilastērion*. Here the sources are meager, and it is not clear how significant the findings are. The usage outside of biblical and Hellenistic Jewish sources is rare. Friedrich Büchsel cites these instances, and in these places the term appears to have the meaning of an oblation (or perhaps propitiation).[22] Within the Old Testament the term (*to hilastērion*, employing the definite article) appears also at Ezek. 43:14, 17, 20 to translate the Hebrew *ázārah* ("ledge"), a part of the altar; blood from a "bull for a sin offering" is to be placed on its four corners for cleansing and atonement (43:20). The term also appears in Philo and Josephus. Philo on occasion describes the *kappōreth* in terms of a "lid (*epithēma*) as a cover (*pōma*) which is called in our holy books *hilastērion"* (*Vit. Mos.* 2.95). Here Philo attests that *hilastērion* was a technical term for the *kappōreth* (as his two other references bear out as well: *Cher.* 25; *Vit. Mos.* 2.97). Josephus uses the term, but not as a technical term for the *kappōreth*. He uses it in connection with a king's building of a memorial as (according to one translation) a "propitiation" of his own terror[23] — or perhaps (according to another proposal) the term is an attributive adjective, so the phrase is to be rendered "a memorial *occasioned* by his fear" (*Ant.* 16.182).[24] The term is also used by Symmachus (late second century A.D.) in his Greek translation of the Old Testament as a translation for the "ark" of Noah (Gen. 6:16), for which no clear explanation (or meaning) can be forthcoming.[25]

There is one other text in which *hilastērion* is used, and which has received considerable attention. That is at 4 Macc. 17:22, in which praises are given to seven brothers who died as martyrs during the persecutions of Antiochus IV Epiphanes:

> [They became] a ransom (*antipsychon*) for the sins of the nation; and through the blood of those righteous ones and their expiatory death (*tou hilastēriou thanatou autōn*), the divine providence delivered (*diesōsen*) Israel, which had suffered evil.[26]

Here the term is used in an adjectival sense, referring to the "expiatory death" of the martyrs. The death of the righteous ones was the means by which the "sins of the nation" were blotted out, and as a consequence God delivered his restored Israel. The book is usually judged to have been written in Greek during the first half of the first century A.D. at Antioch of Syria or Alexandria and therefore contemporaneous with the apostle Paul.[27]

The significance of this particular text and all the other texts cited is assessed in different ways in regard to Paul's usage at Rom. 3:25. It is clear from a review of the debate that theological positions have an effect on the conclusions drawn. It is impossible to do justice here to all the nuances of the debate. At most one can only map out three main positions taken.

First, there are those who continue to hold that at Rom. 3:25 Paul alludes to the *kappōreth* of the Old Testament cultus. Those who hold this view claim that the term *hilastērion* is a neuter noun at Rom.

3:25 (and also in Exodus, Leviticus, and Numbers), and in spite of the problem of Paul's speaking of Christ figuratively as both the one offered and the "place" of atonement at the same time, that is in fact the case. Other New Testament writers mix imagery as well. For example, in the letter to the Hebrews, Jesus is spoken of concurrently as both high priest and the one whose blood is offered in the sacrifice he renders (9:11-14). And in the Fourth Gospel he is both the Lamb of God (1:29, 36) and the Good Shepherd who lays down his life for his sheep (10:11-15). In the Pauline imagery the crucified Christ is the one whom God "put forth" once and for all as the "mercy seat," the place at which atonement is made. Among those who maintain this view of an allusion to the *kappōreth* are H. P. Liddon,[28] Friedrich Büchsel,[29] Adolf Schlatter,[30] Karl Barth,[31] Anders Nygren,[32] T. W. Manson,[33] S. Lyonnet,[34] Joachim Jeremias,[35] Friedrich Lang,[36] F. F. Bruce,[37] Matthew Black,[38] Joseph A. Fitzmyer,[39] Peter Stuhlmacher,[40] W. D. Davies,[41] Hartmut Gese,[42] Martin Hengel,[43] Ulrich Wilckens,[44] Leonhard Goppelt,[45] and Ben F. Meyer.[46] C. K. Barrett holds it as a possibility, but not as a certainty.[47]

The second major position takes *hilastērion* at Rom. 3:25 to signify a "means of propitiation" or "propitiatory sacrifice." According to this point of view, the term is not to be considered a noun — and therefore a direct allusion to the *kappōreth* — but an adjective. The work of Deissmann can be taken as representative. He indicates that on the first occasion the term appears in the Old Testament (Exod. 25:17) it is an adjective (*hilastērion epithēma*). Thereafter, he says, the noun (*epithēma*, "lid" or "cover") was simply dropped, and although one might then conclude that the adjective began functioning as a noun, that is not the case; it retained an adjectival, functional meaning, "propitiatory" (article or thing).[48] When Paul speaks then of Christ as *hilastērion*, he does not have the *kappōreth* in mind (the cross, not Christ, would represent that), but rather his "propitiatory" function. For Paul, Christ crucified is a "means of propitiation." "The crucified Christ is the votive gift of the Divine Love for the salvation of men."[49] Sanday and Headlam write, "There is great harshness, not to say confusion, in making Christ at once priest and victim and place of sprinkling. . . . The Christian *hilastērion* . . . is rather the Cross."[50] When Paul uses the term (an adjective), he therefore thinks of Christ as a "propitiatory sacrifice."[51] Likewise, Leon Morris rejects the view that the apostle alludes to the *kappōreth* or the Day of Atonement ritual, for these, he says, would have had little meaning in Paul's day. Morris makes use of 4 Macc. 17:22 as background which—in his translation—speaks of the death of the martyrs as a "propitiatory death."[52] He writes that, "The wrath of God was conceived of as resting on the people (see II Macc. vii.32–8), and the death of the brothers is viewed as a propitiatory offering which would avail to turn away his wrath."[53] The term *hilastērion* in Rom. 3:25 will also then have to do with "the removal of the wrath of God," and it can be translated "means of propitiation."[54] Others who interpret Rom. 3:25 along these lines include John Murray,[55] David Hill,[56] Herman Ridderbos,[57] C. E. B. Cranfield,[58] and John Piper.[59]

The third major position takes *hilastērion* to signify "expiation" (as the RSV renders it), "means of expiation," "expiation sacrifice," or even "atoning sacrifice." There are various shades of meaning in these terms, and perhaps they cannot all be taken so summarily together. Yet what is common to them is that they move away from the view that *hilastērion* at Rom. 3:25 alludes directly to the *kappōreth* of the Old Testament cultus, while at the same time rejecting the view that Paul speaks of the death of Christ as "propitiating" (appeasing or averting) the wrath of God. God is the subject of the clause, the one who puts forth Christ for the expiation of sin. The work of Dodd is the most decisive for this view in English-speaking scholarship, and it has served as a basis for further work.[60] Dodd examines the verbal cognate of *hilastērion* in the Old Testament (LXX, *hilaskesthai*). He finds that while there are four instances in which the verb (and its compound forms) has the connotation "to propitiate" (Zech. 7:2; 8:22; Mal. 1:9; Ps. 105:30), elsewhere—including every case at which the verb translates Hebrew *kipper*—it has the meaning "to expiate" or "to cleanse from sin or defilement." He writes, "Thus Hellenistic Judaism, as represented by the LXX, does not regard the cultus as a means of pacifying the displeasure of the Deity, but as a means of delivering man from sin, and it looks in the last resort to God to perform that deliverance."[61] In Rom. 3:25, says Dodd, the meaning conveyed by *hilastērion* "(in accordance with the LXX usage, which is constantly determinative for Paul), is that of expiation, not that of propitiation."[62] In his Romans commentary Dodd renders *hilastērion* as "a means by which guilt is annulled."[63]

Likewise others—even if on different grounds—have concluded that at Rom. 3:25 Paul uses the term to signify an "expiation" or "expiatory sacrifice." Eduard Lohse raises four objections (listed in our endnote) to the view that Paul alludes to the *kappōreth;* rather, he says, the background is to be found in 4 Macc. 17:22; the term means "expiatory sacrifice" (German, *Sühnopfer*).[64] Werner G. Kümmel writes that the Roman Christians (mainly gentiles in his view) would not understand an allusion to the *kappōreth*, and he renders the term as "means of expiation" (*Sühnemittel*) or the "means of the reconciling activity of God" (*Mittel des versöhnenden Handeln Gottes*).[65] Ernst Käsemann follows Kümmel and adds, "Jesus could not easily be simultaneously the site of the offering and the offering itself," and suggests as a translation "means of expiation" (*Sühnemittel*).[66] Others to be included in this third group are Heinrich Schlier,[67] Otto Michel,[68] Dieter Zeller,[69] Karl Kertelge,[70], John Knox,[71] J. A. Zeisler,[72] and Gerhard Friedrich.[73]

The interpretation of Rom. 3:25 is thus divided along three basic lines. It is clear that linguistic, historical, and theological matters enter into the picture, and that conclusions are drawn on the basis of what weight a given interpretation places upon each. There has been at least one attempt to resolve the issue by taking a more comprehensive approach. Sam K. Williams concludes that one need not make a choice between "expiation" and "propitiation" (he leaves "mercy seat" out of consideration), since in Hellenistic Judaism (4 Macc. 17:22 particularly) the expiation of sin effects propitation. At Rom. 3:25, he says, *hilastērion* can be understood as "'means of expiation,' but, by implicaton, a means of expiation by which God's wrath is averted so that he is revealed as a gracious Deity."[74] Whether such a proposal can win assent by parties in the dispute is questionable, since positions are held so strongly. Another approach should be taken, and this will be attempted in the next section.

THE IMAGERY RECONSIDERED

In terms of method, it is important to start with the text at hand, and then turn to the question of its background. Part of that back-

ground may be a pre-Pauline formulation. It has been suggested that
all of Rom. 3:24–25 is a pre-Pauline formulation which Paul modified
by his own insertions ("freely by his grace," 3:24; "through faith,"
3:25).[75] Be that as it may, the passage as we have it from the hand
of Paul in Romans has a structure that is not foreign to Paul's usage
elsewhere. Within this structure Paul speaks of God as subject, Christ
as the object, and he makes use of an aorist verb indicating God's putting forth or "sending" his Son for a redemptive purpose.[76] This structure can be seen in the following passages:

> For God has done what the law . . . could not do: having sent
> (*pempsas*) his own Son in the likeness of sinful flesh and for sin, he con-
> demned sin in the flesh.
>
> (Rom. 8:3)
>
> He who did not spare his own Son but gave him up (*paredōken*) for us
> all, will he not also give us all things with him?
>
> (Rom. 8:32)
>
> God sent forth (*exapesteilen*) his Son, born (*genomenon*) of woman,
> born (*genomenon*) under the law, in order to redeem those under the
> law, in order that we might receive adoption as sons.
>
> (Gal. 4:4)

At Rom. 3:24 Paul has already spoken of the redemption (*apolytrōsis*)
which is in Christ. It is in that context that he goes on to say that God
has "put forth publicly" (*proetheto*) his Son as *hilastērion*. Although
it is frequently argued that the verb *proetheto* should be translated
"purposed"[77] — so God "purposed" Christ to be the *hilastērion* — the
sense of "put forth publicly" is more likely in the present context for
three reasons: (1) the construction with a double accusative demands
a verb of action, and not just resolve;[78] (2) the term *protithesthai* is
a cultic term in the LXX for making a public presentation;[79] and (3)
Paul makes use of aorist verbs of action in speaking of God's redemptive work in Christ, as indicated immediately above. The expression
therefore shares the basic structure of the "sending formula." Perhaps
most modern interpreters take the verb to mean "put forth
publicly."[80]

It cannot be emphasized too strongly that in this passage God is
the subject, and that the verb corresponds to those in other passages
cited in which the divine action of sending the Son, or delivering him

to death, for redemption is the focus. Too much has been read into the verb *(proetheto)* in isolation from these verses elsewhere. The result is that interpreters of various persuasions have thought in terms of two stages: (1) God set forth Christ, and (2) Christ offered himself as a sacrifice (either propitiatory or expiatory). But seen within the context of other verbs, this verb speaks of a *singular action* of God in setting forth his Son as *hilastērion;* the Son is entirely passive, the one whom God "set forth" in a particular way for a redemptive purpose. The term *hilastērion* is to be taken as a predicate of the relative pronoun *(hon,* "whom"), referring to Christ. Seen in its totality, with accent on the divine action, what Paul is saying is that God "set forth" the crucified Christ as *hilastērion* (which functions as a noun), which very *action* of setting forth effects atonement. Even the location of the verb at the outset of the clause gives stress to the *action* aspect of the clause.

By paying attention to the structure of the clause, and recognizing its emphasis on the divine action, progress is made in interpretation. First, it must be stressed that the concept of "propitiation" can be dispensed with. The work of Dodd is sufficient in this regard,[81] even though its results have been disputed by those who still insist that (contra Dodd) the passages in which *hilastērion* is used are set within contexts that refer to the anger of God which, they say, must be averted.[82] With Paul, in any case, the stress is totally on the divine activity, not the "work of Christ" over against God. Second, the evidence from 4 Macc. 17:22 pales in its significance. The text speaks of the death of the martyrs as either "expiatory" or "propitiatory"; interpreters are divided on how to render it. In either case, the death of the martyrs themselves has an atoning effect, and the martyrs therefore are redemptive agents in an active sense. But, again, in Rom. 3:25 the stress is wholly on the divine activity in setting forth Christ as *hilastērion* "in his blood" (or by his death). The stress is not upon Christ as one whose death "propitiates" or "expiates" in the sense of the martyrdom tradition.[83]

The issue becomes that of a choice between "mercy seat" and "expiation." Here the history of interpretation is instructive. The older view is that Paul alludes to the *kappōreth* at Rom. 3:25. But, as indicated, the Vulgate departed from this in its rendering the term as *propitiationem*, which was followed by the KJV's "propitiation," in spite of Luther and Tyndale. Moreover, in the nineteenth century and continuing into the present there has been a long history of exegesis that has rejected the older view as well. The alternative (e.g., in Weiss, Deissmann, and Sanday-Headlam) was to take the term to refer to Christ as a "propitiatory sacrifice." Yet that has been seen to be unsatisfactory with many interpreters, and a search for an alternative has been necessary. Terms such as "expiation" or "expiatory sacrifice" have been introduced to replace the language of propitiation. But this turn was taken, one can suspect, (1) because the concept of "propitiation" is unsatisfactory, and (2) the concept of "expiation" is the only alternative that can fill the void adequately in order to speak of Christ's death as a means to remove the consequences of sin.

Yet the term "expiation" is not itself without difficulties. First of all, there is no place within our sources (LXX or nonbiblical Greek) at which *hilastērion* can be translated "expiation." Rom. 3:25 would be an anomaly at this point. Second, the term "expiation" (for *hilastērion*) is a theological construct derived from its associations with the verb *hilaskesthai* (and its compounds). Finally, when the verb *hilaskesthai* is used in the LXX to signify "to expiate," the subject of the verb is human agents, for in the Old Testament it is not God who expiates (or makes atonement), but *persons* who do so. In those cases at which God is the subject of the verb, there is a different meaning—"to be merciful," "to forgive," etc.[84] To be consistent with the meaning of the verb *hilaskesthai* as background for *hilastērion*, the interpreter would have to render Rom. 3:25 as "whom God put forth as a means of displaying his mercy," which no interpreter is prepared to propose. Since it is human agents who "expiate" sin in the Old Testament, not God himself, it would be anomalous to have God as the one who offers an "expiation" at Rom. 3:25. The word "expiation" must therefore come under suspicion as a term that has been used to replace "propitiation" in reaction against a concept foreign to the Bible in general and Pauline theology in particular, but the term is a theological construct that fails to come to terms with the dynamics of expiation: human agents expiate sin. But at Rom. 3:25 the accent is totally on God's action of putting forth Christ for a redemptive purpose.

We are left, then, with the typological interpretation of the ancient fathers, Luther, Tyndale, Calvin (with some uncertainty), and many since: at Rom. 3:25 there is an allusion to the *kappōreth* of Exodus 25 and Leviticus 16, and that can be seen to be a great gain theologically. It has been said that there would be great difficulty for Paul's readers (especially gentiles) to associate the term *hilastērion* with the Old Testament *kappōreth*.[85] If that is so, we must be absolutely frank: it is then more likely that they would have associated the word with its Hellenistic usage, signifying "propitiation," "oblation," or "votive gift" to God.[86] Without the aid of modern theological dictionaries, it is not likely that readers would have thought that, in order to understand this rather strange word, they must trace its etymology to the LXX verb *hilaskesthai*, and specifically to the meaning "to expiate."

Over against the objection that Paul's readers would not have understood *hilastērion* as an allusion to the *kappōreth*, it must be said that that is the most likely understanding they would have had. Paul assumes that at least some of his readers knew the Old Testament, particularly the Torah (cf. Rom. 7:1, "I am speaking to those who know the law"; cf. also 4:1). The Roman community would have been comprised in part of Jewish Christians and gentiles who (as former God-fearers) had become familiar with the Torah in the synagogue.[87] Such persons would be familiar with Leviticus 16 in connection with the Day of Atonement, for the text was read in the synagogues annually on the Day of Atonement throughout the Diaspora.[88] Therefore it would not have been too much for Paul to expect his readers to recall the *kappōreth/hilastērion* of Leviticus 16 at Rom. 3:25, particularly since the clause also contains the words "by his blood." If Paul can make allusions to the Old Testament and Jewish institutions when writing to the primarily gentile Christians at Corinth (cf. 1 Cor. 5:7; 10:1–11; 2 Cor. 3:6–16), it would seem that he would be able to do so all the more when addressing the mixed (Jewish-gentile) community at Rome. Moreover, the usage of Philo and Heb. 9:5 demonstrates that *hilastērion* as *kappōreth* was not lost in first-century Judaism and Christianity.

Finally, it must be said that the other objections raised against this understanding are not strong enough to withstand it. First, the LXX rendering of *kappōreth* at Exod. 25:17 (the first instance of the term in the Old Testament) is *hilastērion epithēma*, but elsewhere it is only *hilastērion*. This fact has caused interpreters, beginning with Deissmann,[89] to say that *hilastērion* is an adjective and that the equivalent for *kappōreth* is actually *epithēma*. But Manson has shown that the term *epithēma* is suspect (as a possible variant) in the textual history of the LXX, and that it was probably first written into the margin (as an explanation, indicating that the *hilastērion* was an *epithēma*, "cover") and then transferred to the text, so *hilastērion* is the noun originally used for *kappōreth*.[90] Second, too much has been made of the point that if Paul wanted to allude to the *kappōreth* of the Old Testament, he should have included the definite article *(to)*, which always appears (except at Exod. 25:17) in the LXX. This point is insisted upon, for example, by Morris and Lohse.[91] But as in the case of the New Testament generally, Paul does not use the definite article before a noun in predicate position.[92]

THE CRUCIFIED CHRIST
AS THE MERCY SEAT

That *hilastērion* in Rom. 3:25 signifies the Old Testament *kappōreth* fits the context of Rom. 3:21–26 well, and it helps to resolve other exegetical difficulties also. It has been suggested that within 3:21–26 Paul makes use of a pre-Pauline tradition. Specifically it has been suggested by some interpreters (but disputed by others) that 3:24–26a is a pre-Pauline confessional formula, into which Paul has inserted "by his grace as a gift" (3:24) and "through faith" (3:25).[93] The formula runs, it is said, through the words "in his divine forebearance," which is 3:26a of the Nestle-Aland Greek text (RSV includes it in 3:25). Among other things, this suggestion helps to overcome the clash between 3:24–26a and the rest of 3:26, which repeats certain words of 3:25.

It is more likely, however, that the so-called insertion within Rom. 3:21–26 is greater in length than this. It can be seen that there is a chiasmus in the Greek text of 3:23–26a. It is not so clear in English, but when the text is presented in Greek it becomes more so. In the schema below, solid lines demonstrate direct correlations, and broken lines show correlations in words sharing common roots or concepts:

A. For all have sinned and fall short of the glory of God
  B. being right-wised freely
    C. by his grace
      D. through the redemption
        E. in Christ Jesus
        E.́ whom God put forth
      D.́ as a mercy seat through faith
    C.́ in his blood
  B.́ for a demonstration of his righteousness
A.́ for the remission of sins committed formerly in the forbearance of God.

A. πάντες γὰρ ἥμαρτον καὶ ὑστεροῦνται τῆς δόξης τοῦ θεοῦ
  B. δικαιούμενοι δωρεὰν
    C. τῇ αὐτοῦ χάριτι
      D. διὰ τῆς ἀπολυτρώσεως
        E. τῆς ἐν Χριστῷ Ἰησοῦ
        E.́ ὃν προέθετο ὁ θεὸς
      D.́ ἱλαστήριον διὰ πίστεως
    C.́ ἐν τῷ αὐτοῦ αἵματι
  B.́ εἰς ἔνδειξιν τῆς δικαιοσύνης αὐτοῦ
A.́ διὰ τὴν πάρεσιν τῶν προγεγονότων ἁμαρτημάτων ἐν τῇ ἀνοχῇ τοῦ θεοῦ.

What is given here is by no means a perfect chiastic structure when it is compared to certain texts of the Old Testament at which the ideal pattern is given (e.g., Ps. 3:7–8 or Isa. 55:7–8), but it is conformed to the pattern as much as chiastic structures are generally in the New Testament and in the Pauline letters particularly, as these are illustrated by Nils W. Lund[94] and Jeremias,[95] although neither has included Rom. 3:23–26a among his examples. Paul's use of the structure is by no means rigid, but consists in a correlation of concepts. He did not employ "rigid rhetorical rules, for the rules became an unconscious equipment in the degree that they have been mastered."[96] The chiastic structure is frequently at best a matter of content, single words, or parts of a sentence in the letters of Paul.[97]

The features of the chiastic structure can be seen in this passage. Lund has summarized the "laws of chiastic structures,"[98] and several of these can be seen to be operative in the structure of Rom. 3:23–26a. First, "the centre is always the turning point." So there is a center in

this passage (E, E' above) which is the turning point, and from that
center there appear two systems (A-D and D'-A') which correspond
roughly in an inverted order. Another law is that there is a tendency
to have certain terms gravitate toward certain positions; for example,
divine names gravitate toward the center in the Psalms. So at E and
E' there is reference to God (E') and Christ (in both E and E') within
Rom. 3:23-26a. Another law is that the second system of a chiasmus
seems to have been constructed to match the first. In Rom. 3:23-26a
the first system (A-E) is constructed in a way that is relatively easy
to follow. It is in the second system (E'-A') that the syntax is most difficult to follow. It appears to have been written to correspond to the
first system, having a certain artificial structure. One may indeed
wish that Paul had composed 3:25-26a (the second system) more
coherently. But when the chiastic structure is seen to exist here, one
can perceive that the section has been composed with deliberation
and skill. Another law is that units are frequently introduced and
concluded with "frame passages." So Rom. 3:23-26a is introduced
(3:21-22) and concluded (3:26b) with passages concerning the
manifestation of the "righteousness of God" in the present (*nuni de*,
"but now," 3:21; *en tō nun kairō*, "at the present time," 3:26b), and
that is the righteousness of God displayed in the crucifixion of Jesus
(3:24-25). Finally, of course, the chiastic structure will have correspondence of ideas and language between the two systems. Linguistic
correspondences have been underscored in the presentation above.
But there are also correspondences in ideas to be seen in C and C' (*tē
autou chariti*, "by his grace" and *ēn tō autou haimati*, "by his blood")
and in D and D' (*apolytrōseōs*, "redemption" and *hilastērion*, "mercy
seat").

Although it has been suggested that Paul employs a pre-Pauline
confessional formula (as indicated above) at Rom. 3:24-26a, another
suggestion can be made. That is that all of Rom. 3:21-26 was composed by Paul, but at more than one stage. Specifically, it can be held
that the chiastic section (3:23-26a) was composed by Paul on an
earlier occasion, and that he employed it in the writing of Romans.
It is difficult to posit a *Sitz im Leben* (life setting) for either the
alleged pre-Pauline formula (3:24-26a) or the larger unit isolated
here (3:23-26a) within the liturgy or hymnody of the early church.[99]

But there is another possibility. That is that the larger unit (3:23–26a) consists of part of a homily that Paul composed and delivered in connection with the Day of Atonement. Subsequently, we shall go on to maintain that other "elements" (not "the transcript" of a complete homily) can be detected in chapter 3 of Romans leading up to 3:23–26a. Its most likely setting would then be that Paul visited a synagogue on the Day of Atonement, and following the lessons for the day, he preached the homily to declare that redemption and forgiveness of sins have now been secured through God's offering of his Son as the *kappōreth*. In the crucified Christ the *kappōreth/hilastērion* has been set forth to manifest the presence of God among his people. Atonement has been made at the "place of atonement," the *kappōreth/hilastērion*, and that "place of atonement" is the crucified, blood-spattered Messiah Jesus.

This suggestion coheres with information available concerning the observance of the Day of Atonement in the synagogues of Paul's day. The synagogue services on this day had a penitential character, containing readings from Scripture, the confession of sins, and prayers for forgiveness.[100] Rabbinic sources—although written in their present form subsequent to Paul's day—preserve the traditional elements. The traditional readings from the Scriptures consisted of those portions of the Torah that institute the day of observance itself (Leviticus 16; Num. 29:7–11), and the readings from the prophets were from Isa. 57:14—58:14; portions of Isaiah 59; Mic. 7:18–20; and the book of Jonah.[101] It has also been suggested that Jer. 8:13—9:24 was read on the day, and that Bar. 3:9—4:4 is a homily based upon it.[102] The readings from the prophets witness to the sins of the people, their need for repentance, and the mercy of God which follows true repentance.

Manson has suggested that Paul wrote his letter to the Romans following a particular Day of Atonement which followed his reconciliation with the church at Corinth, and so the Day of Atonement imagery was in his mind when he wrote Romans (including 3:25).[103] Our own suggestion differs from this. That is that Paul had actually participated in the Day of Atonement in a synagogue prior to writing Romans, and that on that occasion he delivered a homily. Elements of such a homily can be seen in the catena of Scripture passages recited in Rom. 3:10–18. There Paul calls forth passages from the

Psalms and prophets (including Isa. 59:7–8, a traditional text for the Day of Atonement) testifying to human sin according to the custom of the Day of Atonement in the synagogue service. Furthermore, the passage in chiastic structure at Rom. 3:23–26a would have been Paul's conclusion, in which he spelled out the true significance of the day: over against the sinfulness of humanity (3:23), God has now put forth his *kappōreth/hilastērion* through the crucifixion of Jesus, by which atonement has been made. Now the promise of God has been fulfilled—a promise that is repeated as a centerpiece in the traditional passages of the day—given in Lev. 16:30, "for on this day shall atonement be made for you, to cleanse you; from all your sins you shall be clean before the Lord."[104] At this point there would have been division in the synagogue, and Paul may well have been expelled from the service, but also would have been followed by persons interested in hearing him further—the pattern attested in Acts (13:42–43; 17:4, 17–20; 18:5–8).

The Day of Atonement service for which such a homily would have been prepared would not have taken place in Corinth (where Romans was written; cf. Rom. 15:25; Acts 20:2–3); Paul was there for three months during the spring,[105] whereas the Day of Atonement falls in the autumn. But prior to his time in Corinth, Paul had spent two years and three months at Ephesus (Acts 19:8, 10) where both Jews and gentiles heard him. It is most likely at Ephesus that the homily would have been delivered.

That Paul has resorted to the use of one of his own homilies at this point can be held on the basis of other observations concerning the composition of his letters. It has been recognized that the catena of Scripture passages in Rom. 3:10–18 is a unit that has been composed with great care, and that has models in earlier and contemporary Jewish literature.[106] It has been suggested that Paul wrote Rom. 1:18–3:19 as a sustained theological exposition to present God's "case" (or indictment) against the world, incorporating the catena.[107] At the level of composition of the letter to the Romans that is a fitting suggestion.

It has also been recognized that on occasion Paul resorted to the use of homilies in the writing of his letters, and that principle can be applied here. Specifically it has been shown that Paul has incorporated materials from previous homilies at Gal. 3:6–29 and Rom. 4:1–27,[108] as well as in 1 Corinthians 1–3.[109] Such homiletical materials typically have a threefold structure.[110] First, there is a correspondence between the opening and closing statements. At Rom. 3:10 Paul (quoting Eccles. 7:20) writes, "None is righteous (*dikaios*)," which has correspondence in the exposition, "all have sinned and fall short of the glory of God" (3:23) and are justified or made righteous (*dikaioumenoi*) by God's grace through the redemption that is in Christ (3:24). Second, subordinate scriptural quotations supplement the original one; this occurs in 3:11–18. Third, key words or phrases from the opening and/or subordinate quotations are paraphrased in the homily. This happens not only with the word *dikaios* (3:10), which has a correspondence in 3:24, but also with the *pantes* (all) of 3:12, which is reproduced at 3:23. There are also some loose connections – but these are not to be pressed – between the word *haima* ("blood") in 3:15 and 3:25, and also between "the fear of God" in 3:18 and "the glory of God" at 3:23. While the third feature of the homiletical pattern is not so clear, the other two features are clearly present. The form so identified has been called the "homily Gattung."[111] More precisely, one could speak of the form as that of a "midrashic homily."[112]

It must be granted that at the time of writing Romans, Paul worked with considerable freedom. But that freedom would have allowed him to use compositions of his own which had been prepared for other occasions. Chapter 3 of Romans contains an artfully constructed catena of scriptural passages (3:10–18) and a chiastic section (3:23–26a) which, in turn, contains a heavy concentration of unusual terminology (above all, *hilastērion*, but other terms as well; see below). These sections of chapter 3 bear the marks of prior composition in connection with the Day of Atonement, using the imagery for that day (again, *hilastērion* in particular) and resorting to the traditional practice of that day in setting forth the witness of the Scriptures to indict one's hearers of sin and to demonstrate their need for repentance. There may be additional elements in Romans 1–3 drawn from earlier compositions, but at least these two sections (3:10–18, 23–26a) bear such marks. The three chapters were of course composed in their present form on the occasion of writing the letter, but that they contain some prior compositions appears clear.

When Rom. 3:23-26a is seen to be a portion of a homily delivered by Paul on the Day of Atonement, light is shed on various perplexities within it. These can be itemized.

(1) Verse 26b repeats a portion of 3:25, and therefore exegetes have claimed that there is a "seam" to be detected between these verses. Usually it has been said that Paul has employed a pre-Pauline formula in 3:24-26a, and that he resumed his own composition at 3:26b. The same principle (that a seam exists) applies with the suggestion of a chiastic structure ending at 3:26a, except that the unit is now 3:23-26a, rather than 3:24-26a, and that that too is a Pauline composition, albeit at a stage prior to writing Romans.

(2) While the larger unit (3:21-26) shows a "seam" between 3:26a and the rest of the verse, it is not so clear where the former "seam" would be at the outset. Those who propose here a pre-Pauline formula discern the prior "seam" to be between 3:23 and 3:24. But there is difficulty in that, since 3:24 is a dependent clause (beginning with a Greek participle, *dikaioumenoi*, "being justified"), depending for its subject and main clause on 3:23. It is better to include 3:23 with the unit for several reasons. First, it provides the subject ("all"). Second, it initiates a series of main verbs, which are in aorist tense ("sinned," "put forth," and "committed formerly") — a shift in tense over against 3:21-22 — which can be accounted for if this unit was composed previously. Third, 3:23 provides the first member of a chiastic structure. And fourth, the correspondence between 3:21-22 and 3:26b — both attesting to the manifestation of the righteousness of God in the present ("now," 3:21 and "at the present time," 3:26b) — can be seen then to frame the chiastic structure of 3:23-26a. In fact these verses expand the chiastic structure at the level of the composition of the letter.

(3) Rom. 3:23-26a contains words that are rare in Paul's writings. The word "redemption" *(apolytrōsis)* in 3:24 appears at Rom. 8:23 and 1 Cor. 1:30; the word "forebearance" *(anochē)* in 3:26a appears also at Rom. 2:4; the word for "demonstration" *(endeixis)* in 3:25 appears at Rom. 3:26; 2 Cor. 8:24; and Phil. 1:28; the verb *protithēmi* (aorist, "put forth") at 3:25 appears at 1:13 as well, but in a different sense ("to intend"); the word for "sins" *(hamartēmata)* in 3:25

appears at 1 Cor. 6:18 (but the usual term, used over fifty times, is the singular, *harartia*, e.g., at Rom. 3:9, 20; 5:12, 13; or its plural, 1 Cor. 15:3, etc.); and the "blood" *(haima)* of Christ is referred to at Rom. 5:9, but otherwise only in connection with the Lord's Supper (1 Cor. 10:16; 11:25, 27).

The use of such rare terminology in so short a section lends some force to the suggestion that Paul made use of a pre-Pauline formula (not composed by the apostle himself).[113] But actually Paul is capable of using such terms; they fall within his linguistic usage. He could have used them himself in composing the unit in its chiastic structure, for the sake of symmetry, and in connection with a homily in a synagogue on the Day of Atonement. This is particularly the case in the use of the (plural) "sins," for the Day of Atonement is a day for confession of particular sins in the synagogue, not for the confession of "sin" in general. The same setting accounts readily for the reference to the "blood" of Christ as the means of atonement (cf. Lev. 16:14–15, 18–19).

(4) Rom. 3:23–26a contains words that do not otherwise appear in the writings of Paul. These (all in 3:25) are *hilastērion, paresis* (remission), and *proginomai* (here, committed formerly). The first appears elsewhere only at Heb. 9:5 in the New Testament; the second appears nowhere else in the New Testament nor in the LXX; the third appears nowhere else in the New Testament, but it appears three times in the LXX (Wisd. of Sol. 19:13; 2 Macc. 14:3; 15:8). We need not repeat the significance of *hilastērion* for the Day of Atonement. But comment needs to be made concerning the other two words. The term *paresis* is unusual. Kümmel has argued that *paresis* means "forgiveness" (not "overlooking" or "passing over"), a virtual synonym for the more familiar *aphesis,* and his judgment can be accepted.[114] The use of this *hapax legomenon* is a part of the basis for saying that a pre-Pauline tradition is being used. But it must be emphasized that nowhere else does Paul himself use the more familiar *aphesis* in his writings.[115] The term *paresis* may therefore have been the choice of the apostle himself in speaking of the forgiveness of sins. There is no more reason to attribute this word to a pre-Pauline writer (or tradition) than to Paul himself. The use of the participial form of the verb *proginomai* to speak of sins "committed formerly" may, as interpreters have sug-

gested,[116] refer to sins committed prior to the sending of Christ, that is, sins committed during the time of God's patience. Then in a homily on the Day of Atonement, Paul would be saying that *now*,[117] since God has put forth his Son, the day of salvation has arrived. Through the presentation of Christ crucified God has made atonement "to demonstrate his righteousness for the remission of sins committed formerly" since the world began, which includes not only the sins of those who have died long ago but also those in the present. By saying this Paul declares that the eschatological forgiveness of sins — the forgiveness to be exercised in the final judgment by the God who is righteous — has been revealed in the present. The Day of Atonement could provide provisional atonement, leaving the full "remission of sins committed formerly" (subsequently and prior to a person's death) to the final judgment (a similar treatment of the Day of Atonement as provisional, always needing repetition, is found in Heb. 9:25–28).[118] But now, says Paul, the remission of sins committed prior to the final judgment has been exercised by God in the display of his righteousness through the death of Christ.

(5) Finally, the force of the preposition *dia* in 3:25 becomes clear. The use of *dia* and the accusative is disputed. Some see it as having the meaning of "through" ("through the forgiveness of sins").[119] But the analogy is Rom. 4:25 where Paul writes that Christ "was put to death *for* (*dia* plus accusative) our trespasses and raised *for* (*dia* plus accusative) our justification."[120] So God demonstrates his righteousness (or saving activity) "*for* the forgiveness of sins" (cf. Isa. 53:5, LXX). The display has one intended effect: the forgiveness of sins.

Paul's homily must then be seen to have continuity with the tradition of the Day of Atonement, but also discontinuity. The catena of Scripture passages serves to witness to the sins of the gathered community. That is traditional. But rather than making a call for repentance, and in a surprising way, Paul reverts to his gospel of the crucified Messiah as the means by which atonement has been secured. In that proclamation is the implicit call to faith in the divine action toward the world in Christ, which is then brought to light in the "by faith" of 3:25. None is righteous; all have sinned. But God has displayed his saving righteousness in putting forth Jesus crucified as the "mercy seat." The forgiveness of sins committed prior to the final

judgment has been exercised; the provisional has become unconditional. It is based not on repentance, but upon the display of the
righteousness of God in Christ.

THE GOSPEL OF
GOD'S ACT IN CHRIST

The theological tradition speaks of the "work of Christ," and various theories of the atonement have been spelled out to speak of it. It
can be assumed too easily that Paul joins the later generations in such
speech. In fact, however, Paul's focus is not so much on the atoning
work of Christ over against the Father, but rather on the divine
activity itself. God has done an act through Christ that is decisive for
humankind.

The phrase "the work of Christ" is itself found only once in Paul,
and there it has a different meaning than usual. At Phil. 2:30 Paul
says that his fellow worker Epaphroditus "nearly died for the work
of Christ, risking his life to complete your service to me." The very
phrase "work of Christ" for Paul, then, signifies the sacrificial work
that a believer performs on behalf of Christ in the world. When
Christian theology speaks of "the work of Christ" in connection with
the atonement, it is oriented to the Gospel of John, in which the
Johannine Jesus speaks of the work that the Father has given him to
accomplish (4:34; 17:4), and that is accomplished finally in his death
on the cross (19:30).

The tradition has so colored the reading of the New Testament that
the Pauline view cannot be seen clearly. Exegesis of Rom. 3:25 is a
case in point. Whenever it is interpreted to signify Christ as one who
does a "work" on behalf of humankind over against God, averting
God's wrath ("propitiation"), the interpretation has imported conceptions foreign to Paul. And the situation is finally not improved
much when the term "expiation" is inserted in place of "propitiation."
Even here either the idea of expiating sacrifice or the idea of the
covering of sin before God is employed.

Paul's atonement imagery is entirely theocentric. God has put
forth Christ as the "mercy seat." The crucified Christ is God's gift and
the confirmation of his promise to forgive sin. The Day of Atonement, for Paul, had taken on a typological and eschatological sig-

nificance. The divine promise concerning the Day of Atonement was given at Lev. 16:30: "For on this day shall atonement be made for you, to cleanse you; from all your sins you shall be clean before the Lord." The tractate in the *Mishnah* concerning the Day of Atonement shows that in ancient times this verse was recalled three times over in prayers uttered by the high priest, reminding God of his solemn promise.[121] The *Mishnah* in its present form is post-Pauline, but one can be certain—because of the prominence of the motif—that it was traditional to recite the promise. The promise, in any case, appears in the context of the Levitical regulations for the day, and it would have been heard during the reading of the Torah on that day. The promise of God that atonement would be made has now been confirmed in the crucified Messiah. The crucified, blood-spattered Messiah is the *kappōreth/hilastērion*/mercy seat at which atonement has been made. And the atonement itself is a divine action—the work of God, not specifically the work of Christ. Gese has expressed the matter well:

> The crucified one represents God enthroned, and unites us with him through the sacrifice of life by the shedding of human blood. God appears to us and becomes accessible to us in the one who was crucified. Atonement is not instituted by humans . . . but . . . by God. . . . Union with God becomes possible, because God appears to us in our present plight, in our suffering, in our existence in *hamartia* [sin]. The curtain in front of the Holy of Holies has been rent in two.[122]

The theocentric character of the atonement is asserted also in other crucial Pauline passages. The subject of the action is God: God "gave [his Son] up for us all" (Rom. 8:32); "for our sake [God] made him to be sin who knew no sin" (2 Cor. 5:21); in the crucified Christ, God "condemned sin in the flesh" (Rom. 8:3); and "God sent forth his Son" (Gal. 4:4). It is true that there are also passages in Paul that speak of Christ as the subject of the action: "the death he died he died to sin, once for all" (Rom. 6:10); "one has died for all; therefore all have died" (2 Cor. 5:14); "while we were still weak, at the right time Christ died for the ungodly" (Rom. 5:6); "while we were yet sinners Christ died for us" (Rom. 5:8); and "Christ redeemed us . . . having become a curse for us" (Gal. 3:13). Yet it can be seen even in these passages that when Christ is spoken of as the subject of the action, his action is not a means of representing humankind before God, nor is it an action toward God. It is an action that has "us" or "the ungodly" as its object. Christ's action is performed in consequence of the prior act, purposed by God, to redeem humankind. In the idiom of the divine passive, Paul writes, "He was put to death for our trespasses and raised for our justification" (Rom. 4:25).[123]

Rom. 3:21–25 sets forth the Pauline gospel in miniature. In so few lines Paul sums up the closing episode of the history of the righteousness of God. The righteousness of God, which is to be manifested with the coming of the Messiah, has now been revealed in the death of Jesus. Further, the blood-spattered, crucified Messiah is the eschatological fulfillment of the promise of God attending the Day of Atonement. It may have been held in some circles of ancient Judaism that the Day of Atonement would survive into the messianic age, since the law pertaining to its observance is called at Lev. 16:34 "an everlasting statute."[124] In any case, for Paul God has now decisively put forth the "Messiah Jesus" (Rom. 3:24) as the *kapporeth/hilasterion* "by his blood" (3:25). In this instance, however, the *kapporeth* is not hidden from view. The Messiah is crucified in the open, and in his death the promise of Lev. 16:30 is confirmed: "For on this day shall atonement be made for you . . . from all your sins you shall be clean before the Lord." Further, the promise, originally given to Israel, is seen to be extended to all persons "through faith" (Rom. 3:25).

The imagery Paul uses sets forth the gospel in a radical way. The tradition of the Day of Atonement declared that God would be present at the *kapporeth*. The *kapporeth* was intended to serve as the throne of God's presence, the throne of the invisible God (Exod. 25:22; Lev. 16:2; Ps. 99:1). The *kapporeth* was to be hidden from view within the holy of holies and approached only by the high priest on the annual Day of Atonement. By use of the imagery of this Day, however—and presumably in a homily first, and then in his letter to the Romans—Paul declared that now the "mercy seat" has been "set forth" by God in the open air at the cross. In Christ crucified we see that the throne of God's presence—where atonement is made—has been set forth in the midst of godless humanity once and for all.

And the benefits of that act are for Jew and gentile alike. This is made clear by Paul's use of the phrase "by faith" (Rom. 3:25). The *kappōreth* of the Crucified is the antitype and fulfillment of the Israelite institution. The phrase "by faith" signifies that the atonement made here is effective beyond the circle of the children of Abraham "according to the flesh," but is inclusive. As "all have sinned" (3:23), so all are justified freely by the grace of God in Christ (3:24).

But the phrase "by faith" has also been inserted in decisive texts concerning justification. Is there a limitation to the "all-ness" of Rom. 3:23–24 ("all have sinned" and "[all] are justified by his grace")? What is the relationship between justification and "justification by faith"? That is the subject of the next chapter.

NOTES

1. So the section has been called "the centre and heart" of Rom. 1:16b – 15:13 by C. E. B. Cranfield, *A Critical and Exegetical Commentary on the Epistle to the Romans*, ICC (Edinburgh: T. & T. Clark, 1975–79), 199.

2. See below, n. 93.

3. For a discussion of typology, see Gerhard von Rad, "Typological Interpretation of the Old Testament," in *Essays on Old Testament Hermeneutics*, ed. Claus Westermann (Richmond: John Knox Press, 1963), 17–39; idem, *Old Testament Theology* (New York: Harper & Row, 1962–1965) 2:319–429 (esp. pp. 329–35, 364–71); G. W. H. Lampe and K. J. Woolcombe, *Essays on Typology*, SBT 22 (Naperville, Ill.: Alec R. Allenson, 1957); Henry M. Shires, *Finding the Old Testament in the New* (Philadelphia: Westminster Press, 1974), 49–51; Elizabeth Achtemeier, "Typology," *IDBSup*, 926–27; and Leonhard Goppelt, *The Typological Interpretation of the Old Testament in the New* (Grand Rapids: Wm. B. Eerdmans, 1982).

4. The ark was considered the throne of the invisible deity (cf. Num. 10: 35–36). So Martin Noth, *Exodus: A Commentary* (Philadelphia: Westminster Press, 1962), 205; and Hartmut Gese, "The Atonement," in *Essays on Biblical Theology* (Minneapolis: Augsburg Pub. House, 1981), 112–13.

5. von Rad, *Old Testament Theology*, 1:272, writes that the ritual in Leviticus 16 "shows a vast accumulation of expiatory rites." Leviticus 16 (priestly material) gives us a final form of the accumulation. The origins of the various rites connected with the Day of Atonement, however, may be very ancient. Cf. Helmer Ringgren, *Israelite Religion* (Philadelphia: Fortress Press, 1966), 173–74.

6. Origen, *Comm. on Romans*, *Patrologia Graecae*, ed. J. Minge, 14.946a–47b.

7. Eusebius, *Dem. Ev.* 8.2, *Patrologia Graecae*, ed. J. Minge, 22.601D.

8. Theodoret, *Comm. on Romans*, *Patrologia Graecae*, ed. J. Minge, 3.43.

9. John of Damascus, *Comm. on Romans*, *Patrologia Graecae*, ed. J. Minge, 95.465A.

10. Quoted from *Biblia Sacra: Iuxta Vulgatam Versionem*, ed. B. Fischer et al., (Stuttgart: Württembergische Bibelanstalt, 1969), 2:1753.

11. Luther also speaks of Christ as the "mercy seat" (apparently alluding to Rom. 3:25 and Heb. 4:16; 9:5) in his Large Catechism; see *The Book of Concord*, ed. Theodore G. Tappert (Philadelphia: Fortress Press, 1959), 446.

12. Quoted from John Calvin, *Commentaries on the Epistle of Paul the Apostle to the Romans*, trans. and ed. John Owen (Edinburgh: Calvin Translation Society, 1849), 142.

13. *The New Testament*, trans. William Tyndale (1534), ed. N. Hardy Wallis (Cambridge: Cambridge Univ. Press, 1938), 323.

14. Albrecht Ritschl, *Die christliche Lehre von der Rechtfertigung und Versöhnung*, 4th ed. (Bonn: Marcus & Weber, 1900), 2:168–74. The first edition appeared in 1874.

15. E. H. Gifford, *The Epistle to the Romans* (London: Murray, 1868), 91, 96–98.

16. Hermann Cremer, *Biblico-Theological Lexicon of New Testament Greek*, 3d ed. (Gütersloh: G. Bertelsmann, 1900), 305–6.

17. J. A. Bengel, *Gnomon of the New Testament* (Philadelphia: Perkinpine & Higgins, 1888), 2:48–49.

18. Bernhard Weiss, *Der Brief an die Römer*, 8th ed., MeyerK (Göttingen: Vandenhoeck & Ruprecht, 1891), 164–65.

19. Adolf Deissmann, *Bible Studies*, 2d ed. (Edinburgh: T. & T. Clark, 1903), 124–35. The first German edition appeared in 1895.

20. William Sanday and Arthur C. Headlam, *A Critical and Exegetical Commentary on the Epistle to the Romans*, 5th ed., ICC (Edinburgh: T. & T. Clark, 1902), 81, 87–88.

21. Charles H. Dodd, "Hilaskesthai, Its Cognates, Derivatives and Synonymns in the Septuagint," *JTS* 32 (1931):352–60; reprinted as "Atonement" in his book, *The Bible and the Greeks* (London: Hodder & Stoughton, 1935), 82–95. Page references hereafter are to the latter.

22. Friedrich Büchsel, "Hilastērion," *TDNT*, 3:319–20.

23. So it is translated by Allen Wikgren, *Josephus*, LCL (Cambridge, Mass.: Harvard Univ. Press, 1961–81), 8:281.

24. So Büchsel, "Hilastērion," 3:319, n. 10.

25. Ibid., 3:320.

26. The reading is that of Alexandrinus. Sinaiticus reads *tou hilastēriou tou thanatou autōn* (including *tou* as third word, which is absent in Alexandrinus), by which *hilastērion* becomes a noun (so "through the expiation of their death"). The *lectio brevior* of Alexandrinus is to be preferred. Cf. Henry B. Swete, *The Old Testament in Greek According to the Septuagint*

(Cambridge: Cambridge Univ. Press, 1930), 2:760; Büchsel, "Hilastērion," 3:319, n. 7; Peter Stuhlmacher, "Zur neueren Exegese von Röm 3,24–26," in *Jesus und Paulus: Festschrift für Werner Georg Kümmel zum 70. Geburtstag,* ed. E. Earle Ellis and Erich Grässer (Göttingen: Vandenhoeck & Ruprecht, 1975), 327; Heinrich Schlier, *Der Römerbrief,* HTKNT 6 (Freiburg: Herder, 1977), 110; and Ulrich Wilckens, *Der Brief an die Römer,* EKKNT 6 (Köln: Benzinger; Neukirchen-Vluyn: Neukirchener, 1978–82), 1:192. RSV translates the line: "their death as an expiation." The translation of R. B. Townshend in *APOT* 2:683 is "the propitiation of their death" (after Sinaiticus). Sinaiticus is also the reading of *Septuaginta,* ed. Alfred Rahlfs, 7th ed. (Stuttgart: Württembergische Bibelanstalt, 1935), 1:1182.

27. Cf. Leonhard Rost, *Judaism Outside the Hebrew Canon: An Introduction to the Documents* (Nashville: Abingdon Press, 1976), 107–10; George W. E. Nickelsburg, *Jewish Literature between the Bible and the Mishnah* (Philadelphia: Fortress Press, 1981), 223–27.

28. H. P. Liddon, *Explanatory Analysis of St. Paul's Epistle to the Romans,* 2d ed. (London: Longmans, Green & Co., 1893), 75.

29. Büchsel, "Hilastērion," 3:320–23.

30. Adolf Schlatter, *Gottes Gerechtigkeit: Ein Kommentar zum Römerbrief,* 2d ed. (Stuttgart: Calwer, 1952), 148.

31. Karl Barth, *The Epistle to the Romans* (London: Oxford Univ. Press, 1933), 104–5.

32. Anders Nygren, *Commentary on Romans* (Philadelphia: Fortress Press, 1949), 156–58; idem, "Christus, der Gnadenstuhl," in *In Memoriam Ernst Lohmeyer,* ed. W. Schmauch (Stuttgart: Evangelisches Verlagswerk, 1951), 89–93.

33. T. W. Manson, "Hilastērion," *JTS* 46 (1945):1–10.

34. S. Lyonnet, "De notione expiationis," *VD* 37 (1959):336–52.

35. Joachim Jeremias, *The Central Message of the New Testament* (Philadelphia: Fortress Press, 1981), 36.

36. Friedrich Lang, "Gesetz und Bund bei Paulus," in *Rechtfertigung: Festschrift für Ernst Käsemann zum 70. Geburtstag,* ed. J. Friedrich, W. Pöhlmann, and P. Stuhlmacher (Tübingen: J. C. B. Mohr [Paul Siebeck], 1976), 309.

37. F. F. Bruce, *The Epistle of Paul to the Romans,* TNTC (London: Tyndale Press, 1963), 106–7.

38. Matthew Black, *Romans,* NCB (Greenwood: Attic, 1973), 68–70. Black says, however, that this does not exclude the sense of "propitiatory offering."

39. Joseph A. Fitzmyer, *Pauline Theology: A Brief Sketch* (Englewood Cliffs, N.J.: Prentice-Hall, 1967), 44–46.

40. Peter Stuhlmacher, "Zur neueren Exegese von Röm 3,24–26," 315–33; idem, "Sühne oder Versöhnung? Randbemerkungen zu Gerhard Friedrichs Studie: 'Die Verkündigung des Todes Jesu im Neuen Testament,'" in *Die*

Mitte des Neuen Testaments: Einheit und Vielfalt neutestamentlicher Theologie: Festschrift für Eduard Schweizer zum siebzigsten Geburtstag, ed. Ulrich Luz and Hans Weder (Göttingen: Vandenhoeck & Ruprecht, 1983), 300–304.

41. W. D. Davies, "From Tyranny to Liberation: The Pauline Experience of Alienation and Reconciliation," in *Jewish and Pauline Studies* (Philadelphia: Fortress Press, 1984), 212–13.

42. Gese, "The Atonement," 115.

43. Martin Hengel, *The Atonement: The Origins of the Doctrine in the New Testament* (Philadelphia: Fortress Press, 1981), 45.

44. Wilckens, *Römer*, 1:190–96.

45. Leonhard Goppelt, *Theology of the New Testament* (Grand Rapids: Wm. B. Eerdmans, 1981–82), 2:95–97.

46. Ben F. Meyer, "The Pre-Pauline Formula in Rom. 3:25–26a," *NTS* 29 (1983): 198–208.

47. C. K. Barrett, *A Commentary on the Epistle to the Romans*, HNTC (New York: Harper & Brothers, 1957), 78.

48. Deissmann, *Bible Studies*, 125–27.

49. Ibid., 133.

50. Sanday and Headlam, *Romans*, 87.

51. Ibid., 88.

52. Leon Morris, "The Meaning of *Hilastērion* in Romans III.25," *NTS* 2 (1955): 33–43 (esp. p. 40). Cf. also his books, *The Apostolic Preaching of the Cross* (London: Tyndale Press, 1955), 167–74; and *The Cross in the New Testament* (Grand Rapids: Wm. B. Eerdmans, 1965), 225–26.

53. Morris, "Meaning of *Hilastērion*," 42.

54. Ibid., 43.

55. John Murray, *The Epistle to the Romans* (Grand Rapids: Wm. B. Eerdmans, 1959–65), 1:116–21.

56. David Hill, *Greek Words and Hebrew Meanings: Studies in the Semantics of Soteriological Terms*, SNTSMS 5 (Cambridge: Cambridge Univ. Press, 1967), 38–48.

57. Herman Ridderbos, *Paul: An Outline of His Theology* (Grand Rapids: Wm. B. Eerdmans, 1975), 187.

58. Cranfield, *Romans*, 214–18.

59. John Piper, "The Demonstration of the Righteousness of God in Romans 3:25, 26," *JSNT* 7 (1980): 31.

60. Dodd, *Bible and the Greeks*, 82–95.

61. Ibid., 93.

62. Ibid., 94.

63. Charles H. Dodd, *The Epistle of Paul to the Romans*, MNTC (New York: Harper & Brothers, 1932), 55.

64. Eduard Lohse, *Märtyrer und Gottesknecht: Untersuchungen zur urchristlichen Verkündigung vom Sühntod Jesu Christi*, FRLANT 46, new

series (Göttingen: Vandenhoeck & Ruprecht, 1955), 15–53. The four reasons
are: (1) Paul does not explicitly indicate to his readers that he has the *kappō-reth* in mind; (2) Paul does not use the definite article *(to)*, which is always
found in the LXX (except in Exod. 25:17); (3) Paul speaks of God's presenting
(proetheto) Christ publicly, while the *kappōreth* was hid from view; and (4)
it would be the cross, not Christ, that would correspond to the *kappōreth*.

65. Werner G. Kümmel, "Paresis und Endeixis: Ein Beitrag zum Verständnis der paulinischen Rechtfertigungslehre," *ZTK* 49 (1952):160.

66. Ernst Käsemann, *Commentary on Romans* (Grand Rapids: Wm. B.
Eerdmans, 1980), 97; German text: *An die Römer*, 4th ed., HNT 8a (Tübingen: J. C. B. Mohr [Paul Siebeck], 1980), 91.

67. H. Schlier, *Römerbrief*, 110–11.

68. Otto Michel, *Der Brief an die Römer*, 11th ed., MeyerK 4 (Göttingen:
Vandenhoeck & Ruprecht, 1957), 92–93.

69. Dieter Zeller, "Sühne und Langmut: Zur Traditionsgeschichte von
Röm 3, 24–26," *Theologie und Philosophie* 43 (1968):54–57.

70. Karl Kertelge, *"Rechtfertigung" bei Paulus*, NTAbh, Neue Folge 3
(Münster: Aschendorf, 1967), 55–58.

71. John Knox, *Romans, Interpreter's Bible*, ed. G. Buttrick (Nashville:
Abingdon Press, 1952–57), 9:432–33.

72. J. A. Zeisler, "Romans 3:21–26," *ExpTim* 93 (1982):358. Yet Zeisler sets
forth a modified view that ends up being participationist and moralistic:
"The cross then is God's means of dealing with sin in enabling believers to
die to it."

73. Gerhard Friedrich, *Die Verkündigung des Todes Jesu im Neuen Testament*, Biblisch-Theologische Studien 6 (Neukirchen-Vluyn: Neukirchener,
1982), 60–67.

74. Sam K. Williams, *Jesus' Death as Saving Event: The Background and
Origin of a Concept*, HDR 2 (Missoula, Mont.: Scholars Press, 1975), 38–41;
the quotation is from p. 40.

75. For discussion of this, see "The Crucified Christ as the Mercy Seat"
below and for bibliography see n. 93.

76. This is also expressed in the divine passive at Rom. 4:25: "Jesus our
Lord, who was delivered *(paredothē)* for our trespasses and raised *(ēgerthē)*
for our justification." Concerning the pre-Pauline origin and Pauline use of
the "sending" formula in Rom. 4:25; 8:3, 32; and Gal. 4:4, see Werner
Kramer, *Christ, Lord, Son of God*, SBT 50 (Naperville, Ill.: Alec R. Allenson,
1966), 112–19, 186–89.

77. Cranfield, *Romans*, 208–9 (with further references); the analogy is
Rom. 1:13.

78. Christian Maurer, *Protithēmi*," *TDNT*, 8:165–66. Cf. C. F. D. Moule,
An Idiom-Book of New Testament Greek, 2d ed. (Cambridge: Cambridge
Univ. Press, 1960), 35.

79. Stuhlmacher, "Zur neueren Exegese von Röm 3,24–26," 328; Wilckens,
Römer, 1:192. These interpreters point to the following LXX passages: Exod.

29:23; 40:23; Lev. 24:8; 2 Macc. 1:8, 15.

80. Sanday and Headlam, *Romans*, 87; Manson, *"Hilastērion,"* 5; Morris, "The Meaning of *Hilastērion* in Romans III.25," 42; Murray, *Romans*, 1.118; Nygren, *Romans*, 158–59; Michel, *Römer*, 88, 92; Barrett, *Romans*, 77; Bruce, *Romans*, 107; Käsemann, *Romans*, 97; and Wilckens, *Römer*, 1.192.

81. Dodd, *Bible and the Greeks*, 82–95.

82. Morris, "Meaning of *Hilastērion* in Romans III.25," 33–43; Hill, *Greek Words and Hebrew Meanings*, 38–48.

83. Cf. D. E. H. Whiteley, *The Theology of St. Paul* (Oxford: Basil Blackwell, 1964), 146–48.

84. Cf. Dodd, *Bible and the Greeks*, 82–95; this is confirmed by the more recent study of K. Grayston, *"Hilaskesthai* and Related Words in the LXX," *NTS* 27 (1981):647–48. Moreover, in the Dead Sea Scrolls the term *kipper* appears with God as the subject, and the meaning is that of to "forgive" or "pardon." For texts and discussion, see Helmer Ringgren, *The Faith of Qumran* (Philadelphia: Fortress Press, 1963), 121–22; and E. P. Sanders, *Paul and Palestinian Judaism: A Comparison of Patterns of Religion* (Philadelphia: Fortress Press, 1977), 298–305.

It has been said that "when expiation is not linked with the cultus, it is usually a direct act of God," who does the expiating, and so the "sin or offense . . . is thus 'covered' . . . by God himself," R. Abba, "Expiation," *IDB*, 2:200. Abba then cites Ps. 32:1; 51:9; Isa. 43:25; 44:22; and Jer. 18:23. It is significant, however, that the Hebrew *kipper* is not rendered in the LXX by the verb *hilaskesthai* in these instances, but by the verbs *epikalyptō* ("to cover," LXX, Ps. 31:1), *exaleiphō* ("to wipe out" or "to blot out," LXX, Ps. 50:11; Isa. 43:25; Jer. 18:23), or *apaleiphō* ("to wipe away," Isa. 44:22).

85. Among others, cf. Deissmann, *Bible Studies*, 129; Sanday and Headlam, *Romans*, 87; Morris, "The Meaning of *Hilastērion* in Romans III.25," 40–41; and Cranfield, *Romans*, 215.

86. This is the rendering of Deissmann, *Bible Studies*, 133.

87. On the Jewish and gentile Christian composition of the Roman community, see Werner G. Kümmel, *Introduction to the New Testament*, rev. ed. (Nashville: Abingdon Press, 1975), 309–10; and Günther Bornkamm, *Paul* (New York: Harper & Row, 1971), 89–90.

88. Cf. *m. Yoma* 5:3–4; Str-B, 3.179–90; Theodor H. Gaster, *Festivals of the Jewish Year* (New York: William Sloane, 1952), 146–51; Moshe D. Herr, "Day of Atonement," *EncJud*, 5:1376–84. Further discussion is provided by Manson, *"Hilastērion,"* 6–7; and Wilckens, *Römer*, 1:191.

89. Deissmann, *Bible Studies*, 125–26.

90. Manson, *"Hilastērion,"* 3. Cf. W. D. Davies, *Paul and Rabbinic Judaism: Some Rabbinic Elements in Pauline Theology*, 4th ed. (Philadelphia: Fortress Press, 1980), 240.

91. Morris, "The Meaning of *Hilastērion* in Romans III.25," 35; Lohse, *Märtyrer und Gottesknecht*, 151.

92. Cf. BDF #252 (p. 132); J. H. Moulton, *A Grammar of New Testament*

Greek (Edinburgh: T. & T. Clark, 1906–76), 3:183; Stuhlmacher, "Zur neueren Exegese von Röm 3, 24–26," 322–23; idem, "Sühne oder Versöhnung?" 303–4; and Wilckens, *Römer*, 1:191.

93. Rudolf Bultmann, *Theology of the New Testament* (New York: Charles Scribners' Sons, 1951–55), 1:46; Ernst Käsemann, "Zum Verständnis von Römer 3, 24–26," *ZNW* 43 (1950/51):150–54; idem, *Romans*, 96–99; Michel, *Römer*, 89; A. M. Hunter, *Paul and His Predecessors*, rev. ed. (Philadelphia: Westminster Press, 1961), 120–122; Peter Stuhlmacher, *Gerechtigkeit Gottes bei Paulus*, FRLANT 87 (Göttingen: Vandenhoeck & Ruprecht, 1965), 86–91; idem, "Zur neueren Exegese von Röm 3, 24–26," 315–16; Hans Conzelmann, *An Outline of the Theology of the New Testament* (New York: Harper & Row, 1969), 166; Kertelge, *"Rechtfertigung" bei Paulus*, 48–62; and Werner G. Kümmel, *The Theology of the New Testament* (Nashville: Abingdon Press, 1973), 198. A survey of the German discussion is provided by John Reumann, "The Gospel of the Righteousness of God: Pauline Reinterpretation in Romans 3:21–31," *Int* 20 (1966):432–52; cf. also idem, *"Righteousness" in the New Testament: "Justification" in the United States Lutheran-Roman Catholic Dialogue* (Philadelphia: Fortress Press, 1982), 36–38.

Wilckens, *Römer*, 1:183, attributes 3:25–26a (excluding 3:24) to pre-Pauline tradition. The same is true of Lohse, *Märtyrer und Gottesknecht*, 149–50; and Meyer, "Pre-Pauline Formula in Rom. 3.25–26a," 198–208. It has also been argued that 3:25–26 (so excluding 3:24) is a non-Pauline fragment, but that this is a later (post-Pauline) interpolation: Charles H. Talbert, "A Non-Pauline Fragment at Romans 3:24–26?" *JBL* 85 (1966):287–96.

Finally, it has been argued that only 3:25 (and not all of that) is a pre-Pauline tradition: Georg Strecker, "Befreiung und Rechtfertigung. Zur Stellung der Rechtfertigungslehre in der Theologie des Paulus," in *Rechtfertigung*, ed. J. Friedrich, W. Pöhlmann, and P. Stuhlmacher, 501–2.

On the other hand, various interpreters take the passage to be a Pauline composition: Otto Kuss, *Der Römerbrief* (Regensburg: F. Pustet, 1957 –), 1:160–61; S. Lyonnet, "Notes sur l'exegèsè de l'Épître aux Romains," *Bib* 38 (1957):59; Schlier, *Römerbrief*, 107, n. 8; and Cranfield, *Romans*, 200, n. 1. Zeisler, *The Meaning of Righteousness*, 192–94, 209–10, works on the assumption that the passage is Pauline, but grants that "something like Käsemann's view is not implausible" (p. 210).

94. Nils W. Lund, *Chiasmus in the New Testament: A Study in Formgeschichte* (Chapel Hill: Univ. of North Carolina Press, 1942), 139–225.

95. Joachim Jeremias, "Chiasmus in den Paulusbriefen," *ZNW* 49 (1958), 145–56.

96. Lund, *Chiasmus in the New Testament*, 208.

97. Jeremias, "Chiasmus in den Paulusbriefen," 145. He illustrates from various texts on pp. 145–52. Other studies on chiasmus in Paul's letters include John J. Collins, "Chiasmus, the 'ABA' Pattern and the Text of Paul,"

Studiorum Paulinorum Congressus Internationalis Catholicus, Analecta Biblica 17–18 (Rome: Pontifical Biblical Institute, 1963), 2:575–83; and Kendrick Grobel, "A Chiastic Retribution-Formula in Romans 2," *Zeit und Geschichte: Dankesgabe an Rudolf Bultmann zum 80. Geburtstag,* ed. Erich Dinkler (Tübingen: J. C. B. Mohr [Paul Siebeck], 1964), 255–261.

98. Lund, *Chiasmus in the New Testament,* 40–41.

99. It has been suggested that the *Sitz im Leben* of the alleged "pre-Pauline formula" of Rom. 3:24–26a was either the Lord's Supper or a baptismal liturgy. For the Lord's Supper: Käsemann, "Zum Verständnis von Römer 3, 24–26," 99–100; Stuhlmacher, *Gerechtigkeit,* 88–89; Michel, *Römer,* 92; and Kertelge, *"Rechtfertigung" bei Paulus,* 62. For a baptismal liturgy: Ferdinand Hahn, "Taufe und Rechtfertigung. Ein Beitrag zur paulinischen Theologie in ihrer Vor- und Nachgeschichte," *Rechtfertigung,* ed. J. Friedrich, W. Pöhlmann, and P. Stuhlmacher, 95–124; Strecker, "Befreiung und Rechtfertigung," 502; and Meyer, "Pre-Pauline Formula in Rom. 3.25–26a," 206.

100. George Foot Moore, *Judaism in the First Centuries of the Christian Era* (Cambridge, Mass.: Harvard Univ. Press, 1927–30), 2:55–65; Hayyim Schauss, *Guide to Jewish Holy Days* (New York: Schocken Books, 1938), 125–42; Gaster, *Festivals of the Jewish Year,* 146–51. Penitential prayers are preserved in *m. Yoma* 3:8; 4:2; 6:2.

101. Gaster, *Festivals of the Jewish Year,* 156–65; Herr, "Day of Atonement," *EncJud,* 5:1379.

102. H. St. John Thackeray, *The Septuagint and Jewish Worship: A Study in Origins* (London: Milford, 1921), 95–100.

103. Manson, "Hilastērion," 7–8.

104. This passage from Lev. 16:30 is repeated in each of the prayers recited by the high priest on the Day of Atonement (*m. Yoma* 3:8; 4:2; 6:2).

105. Cf. Kümmel, *Introduction to the New Testament,* 311. He dates Romans to "about the spring of 55 or 56 (according to Acts 20:6, Paul was again in Philippi at Passover)."

106. For a survey of discussion, see Leander E. Keck, "The Function of Rom. 3:10–18: Observations and Suggestions," in *God's Christ and His People: Studies in Honour of Nils Alstrup Dahl,* ed. Jacob Jervell and Wayne A. Meeks (Oslo: Universitetsforlaget, 1977), 141–57.

107. Ibid., 152.

108. Peder Borgen, *Bread from Heaven: An Exegetical Study of the Concept of Manna in the Gospel of John and the Writings of Philo,* NovTSup 10 (Leiden: E. J. Brill, 1965), 47–58.

109. Wilhelm Wuellner, "Haggadic Homily Genre in I Corinthians 1–3," *JBL* 89 (1970):199–204; and Vincent P. Branick, "Source and Redaction Analysis of 1 Corinthians 1–3," *JBL* 101 (1982):251–69.

110. So Borgen, *Bread from Heaven,* 47.

111. Wuellner, "Haggadic Homily Genre," 203. Borgen had called it simply a "homiletic pattern," *Bread from Heaven,* 46, etc.

112. The midrashic character of Pauline materials has also been recognized by E. Earle Ellis, *Prophecy and Hermeneutic in Early Christianity* (Grand Rapids: Wm. B. Eerdmans, 1978), 213–20. On pp. 217–18 Ellis considers Rom. 1:17 – 4:24 as a unit constructed in midrashic form. That would be compatible with our own suggestion but applied at the level of the writing of Romans.

113. Cf. Käsemann, *Romans*, 99.

114. Kümmel, "*Paresis* and *Endeixis*," 3–4. Cf. also Rudolf Bultmann, "*Aphiēmi*," *TDNT*, 1:511–12; Käsemann, *Romans*, 98; Wilckens, *Römer*, 1:196; Nils A. Dahl, "Promise and Fulfillment," *Studies in Paul* (Minneapolis: Augsburg Pub. House, 1977), 129; and Meyer, "Pre-Pauline Formula in Rom. 3.25–26a," 204.

Some interpreters, however, make a distinction between the two nouns, so that *paresis* means a "passing over" (not "remission") of sins: R. C. Trench, *Synonymns of the New Testament*, 9th ed. (London: Macmillan & Co., 1880), 114–19; Sanday and Headlam, *Romans*, 90; H. P. Liddon, *Romans*, 77–78; Cranfield, *Romans*, 211; and Cyril Blackman, "Romans 3:26a: A Question of Translation," *JBL* 87 (1968):203–4.

115. It does appear, however, in the deutero-Paulines: Eph. 1:17; Col. 1:14.

116. W. G. Kümmel, "*Paresis* and *Endeixis*," 11; Käsemann, *Romans*, 98; Stuhlmacher, *Gerechtigkeit*, 89; Michel, *Römer*, 93–94; Wilckens, *Römer*, 1:196; Meyer, "Pre-Pauline Formula in Rom. 3.25–26a," 204–5. Cf. also BAGD, 703.

117. Both the *nuni* of Rom. 3:21 and the *nun* of 3:26 speak of a shift to the eschatological age. Cf. G. Stählin, "*Nun*," *TDNT*, 4:1117; Käsemann, *Romans*, 92; Michel, *Römer*, 89; Cranfield, *Romans*, 201; and Wilckens, *Römer*, 1:184.

118. On the provisional character of the Day of Atonement, see Gaster, *Festivals of the Jewish Year*, 145–46. On the character of forgiveness and justification as eschatological, see G. Schrenk, "*Dikē*," *TDNT*, 2:205.

119. Kümmel, "*Paresis* and *Endeixis*," 10–11; Wilckens, *Römer*, 1:196.

120. Cf. also Rom. 11:28. It has been suggested that already in the New Testament, including Paul, "*dia* is on the way to the meaning 'for' which it has in modern Greek," Maximilian Zerwick, *Biblical Greek* (Rome: Scripta Pontificii Instituti Biblici, 1963), 37. The analogy of Rom. 4:25 is also used by Moule, *Idiom-Book of New Testament Greek*, 55; Moulton, *Grammar of New Testament Greek*, 3:268; and Meyer, "Pre-Pauline Formula in Rom. 3.25–26a," 204.

121. See *m. Yoma* 3:8; 4:2; 6:2. Cf. also 8:9.

122. Gese, "The Atonement," 115.

123. Two passages in Paul may be cited as instances of Christ's representing us before God: "we shall be saved by him from the wrath of God" (Rom. 5:9) and that in which Paul says that Christ "intercedes for us" (Rom. 8:34). But these passages are set within the context of declaring God's love for us

in Christ (Rom. 5:8; 8:39), our rejoicing in God (Rom. 5:11), and the good news that "it is God who justifies" (Rom. 8:33).

124. W. D. Davies, *Torah in the Messianic Age and/or Age to Come*, JBLMS 11 (Philadelphia: Society of Biblical Literature, 1952), 56–57. Davies cites from *Yalquṭ* on Prov. 9:2, which relates a saying of Rabbi Eleazar (second generation of rabbinic teachers, A.D. 80–120).

4. Justification of Humanity and Justification by Faith

It is curious that in the history of Pauline studies it has been routinely assumed that all of what Paul says concerning "justification" can be exhausted under the topic of "justification by faith." The matter is curious, for it is simply a fact that Paul speaks on occasion about justification apart from using the full phrase "justification by faith." Methodologically it seems that justification should be treated as a general concept prior to the particular concept of justification by faith. Moreover, justification should be treated within the context of the larger panorama of Paul's theology. Only then — after justification has been explored in general, and has been placed within the context of Paul's theology — should the more specialized term "justification by faith" be taken up.

It has become increasingly recognized in modern times that justification is only one of the Pauline metaphors concerning the effects of God's action toward the world through Christ. The corollary is sometimes drawn that justification has been emphasized too much, especially in Protestant interpretations of Paul. Yet the language of justification is strikingly frequent in Paul's letters, and the sheer frequency alone calls for attention.

In his undisputedly authentic letters the apostle uses the verb "to justify" (*dikaioō*) — in the sense of justification before God — twenty-five times.[1] Although he uses the term "justification" (*dikaiōsis*) only twice,[2] he speaks of the bestowing, reckoning, or gaining of "righteousness" (*dikaiosynē*) — again, in the sense of being justified before God — some twenty-one times.[3] This usage surpasses even the language of "salvation." Paul uses the verb "to save" (*sōzō*) nineteen times,[4] and he uses the term "salvation" (*sōtēria*) fourteen times.[5]

Other terms, by comparison, are used relatively little. The verb "to reconcile" (*katallassō*) appears five times,[6] and the noun "reconciliation" (*katallagē*) four times.[7] The verb "to redeem" (*exagorazō*) appears twice,[8] and the noun "redemption" (*apolytrōsis*) appears three times.[9]

Although the full phrase "justification by faith" is used frequently enough in Paul's letters (Rom. 3:26–30; 5:1; 10:4; Gal. 2:16; 3:8, 24; Phil. 3:9) to demand attention, the apostle also speaks of justification several times apart from the full phrase, as the following passages demonstrate (all from Romans): "Since all have sinned and fall short of the glory of God, they are justified by his grace as a gift through the redemption which is in Christ Jesus" (3:24–25); "[Christ] was put to death for our trespasses and raised for our justification" (4:25); "Since, therefore, we are now justified by his blood, much more shall we be saved by him from the wrath of God" (5:9); "Then as one man's trespass led to condemnation for all persons, so one man's act of right-eousness leads to justification resulting in life for all persons" (5:18); and "It is God who justifies" (8:33).

The question must be asked, in light of these passages, whether the language of justification in Paul might be used in two contexts, each having a place of its own in his theology. Is there a doctrine of justification, which stresses the divine action — flowing from the righteousness of God — as well as the more common theme of justification by faith, which stresses the anthropological side of Paul's theological outlook?[10] The contention of this chapter is that such is the case.

That justification is used by Paul in two senses for different contexts should not be surprising, for there is a parallel to it in his statements concerning reconciliation. On the one hand, Paul writes that "in Christ God was reconciling the world to himself, not counting their trespasses against them" (2 Cor. 5:19). Here Paul stresses totally the action of God toward the world in Christ — a deed done. The world is reconciled to God, and the "trespasses" of humanity are no longer counted, even prior to and apart from faith.[11] On the other hand, Paul — as one entrusted with the message of reconciliation — exhorts his readers to "be reconciled to God" (2 Cor. 5:20). Here Paul stresses that, on the basis of the divine action, believers are to accept the fact of their having been reconciled and to be at peace with God. The

anthropological aspect now comes to the fore. Justification and
reconciliation are closely linked together in Paul's thinking.[12] In Rom.
5:9 Paul speaks of justification through the blood of Christ and then
goes on immediately to speak of being "reconciled to God by the
death of his Son" (5:10), and in 2 Corinthians 5 the discussion of
reconciliation (5:18–20) concludes with a statement on justification
(5:21). If Paul can speak of reconciliation both (1) in terms of a divine
action apart from faith and (2) in terms of human response to the
divine action, it is possible for him (a) to speak of divine justification
of the world apart from faith and (b) to speak of justification by faith
as a related, but not identical, concept.

Elsewhere in Paul's writings other expressions and affirmations are
used as well that speak of God's saving action toward the world apart
from faith on the part of humanity. Most prominent are those passages that employ the *hyper*-formula — many of which may have been
derived from creedal statements — which speak of Christ as having
died, or having been put to death, "for the ungodly" (Rom. 5:6), "for
us" (Rom. 5:8), "for us all" (Rom. 8:32), "for our sins" (1 Cor. 15:3;
Gal. 1:4), "for me" (Gal. 2:20); Christ became in his crucifixion a
curse "for us" (Gal. 3:13).[13] Closely related are the statements of Paul
that God sent his Son "for sin" (*peri hamartias*) and "condemned sin
in the flesh" (Rom. 8:3), and that Christ was put to death "for our
trespasses" (*dia ta paraptōmata hēmōn*, Rom. 4:25) and was raised
"for our justification" (*dia tēn dikaiōsin hēmōn*, Rom. 4:25).

In addition to these statements about the superabundant effects of
Christ's atoning death "for us" or "for our sins," and so on, there are
passages in which Paul looks to the future manifestation of the lordship of God over his entire creation at the Parousia of Christ. The
creation — including humanity[14] — "will be set free from its bondage to
decay and obtain the glorious liberty of the children of God" (Rom.
8:21). God will finally be "everything to everyone" (1 Cor. 15:28). At
the name of Jesus "every knee shall bow" and "every tongue confess"
him as Lord (Phil. 2:10–11) — a passage that (although pre-Pauline
here,[15] but cf. Rom. 14:11) speaks of the eschatological future when
the cosmic lordship of Christ will be recognized by all ("in heaven
and on earth and under the earth"), not simply by those who have
believed in the present age.[16] All peoples and supernatural powers,

including even those who have been hostile, will confess that Jesus is Lord.[17] All Israel will be saved — in spite of unbelief and even rejection of the gospel during historical time — purely by grace, for God's gifts and call are irrevocable (Rom. 11:26–31).[18] Death will be destroyed (1 Cor. 15:51–57). And as in Adam all die, so in Christ shall all be made alive (1 Cor. 15:22; cf. 15:49; Rom. 5:12–21).

The action of God toward the world in Jesus Christ is portrayed in such passages by Paul as so far reaching (or grasping) that no corner of creation is left untouched. This motif came to further expression in one of the deutero-Pauline letters, one of the earliest literary interpretations of Paul, concerning Christ: "For in him all the fulness of God was pleased to dwell, and through him to reconcile all things, whether on earth or in heaven, making peace by the blood of the cross" (Col. 1:19–20). But the motif is already found in Paul. One of its clearest expressions appears in one of his most sweeping statements: "God has consigned all persons to disobedience, in order that he may have mercy on all" (Rom. 11:32).

One can raise the question whether all of these affirmations of Paul can be relegated to "doxological hyperbole" and whether they express thoughts that he did not seriously intend. Yet when we consider that Paul wrote such things in the pre-Constantinian world of the first century, when far less than one percent of the world he knew was Christian — and wrote them in light of an imminent expectation of the Parousia, which would hardly allow for the triumph of Christianity over the face of the globe in history — we cannot think of these expressions as mere idle talk. They are rooted in the prior theological conviction of Paul concerning the righteousness of God, which has now been revealed (Rom. 3:21), and which reaches out to reclaim the fallen creation, no longer computing the trespasses of humanity (2 Cor. 5:19; cf. Rom. 3:25).

Justification of humanity by God through Christ and justification by faith can and ought to be treated as two separate, although related, topics. This becomes evident especially in connection with Rom. 5:12–21. This passage is routinely ignored in a discussion of justification. But the passage is one of the most extensive on the subject.[19] One reason for the lack of attention given to it may be that it nowhere speaks of "justification by faith," and justification is nor-

treated in Pauline studies under the heading of that full phrase. ... passage speaks of eras or segments of history (Adam to Moses, Moses to Christ, and the era of Christ) and of the existence of humankind under Adam and Christ. But it is above all a passage that speaks of the scope of sin and the scope of justification in a rather sustained and thought-out argument.[20] It is therefore essential to an understanding of the Pauline doctrine of justification. Our discussion of justification will begin with this passage, and then proceed to justification by faith against this as a background.

JUSTIFICATION OF HUMANITY

Prior to Rom. 5:12–21, Paul has already established a number of points. He has declared that all humanity stands under the wrath of God, under the power of sin, and is unable to be justified through works of the law (1:18 – 3:20). But God has manifested his righteousness in Christ in order to justify both Jew and gentile on a foundation other than law, and that is his own righteousness, which is received by faith alone as God's justifying power (3:20–31). This claim has a scriptural basis to it in the story of Abraham, who was reckoned righteous by God when he believed the promises of God, even before he was circumcised (i.e., while he was technically a gentile), so it is clear that those who believe the promises of God are, like Abraham, the justified ones (4:1–25). Justified by faith, we have peace with God, and even though that does not preclude suffering in the present, we know that we are justified, reconciled, and saved from the wrath of God for the world to come (5:1–11). At this point Paul breaks off this discussion.

The following section (5:12–21) opens with "therefore" (*dia touto*),[21] which has no clear antecedent. Throughout 5:1–11 Paul has used the first person plural, but now he switches to third person and continues that mode through 5:12–21. He does not merely continue the previous discussion, but uses the "therefore" (5:12) to mark a transition,[22] by which he allows himself to recast his thinking and presentation in light of what has gone before in a new way, and that turns out to be a discussion of the effects of Adam and Christ upon all humanity. Up to this point Paul has established that through God's act of righteousness in Christ there is justification, reconciliation, and final salvation (life) for all who believe. But now he takes a different approach to the matter of "justification" and "life." Without denying or amending what has already been said, he goes on to treat justification and life under the broader horizons of their theocentric origins. There is a change of models. While the earlier discussion was based on the situation of humankind before God, and taking issue with the claims of those who would argue for justification before God through works of the law, now his discussion is based on the apocalyptic view of the ages. The forensic model gives way to an apocalyptic one. The situation of humanity under the wrath of God has been altered in the new aeon, which has dawned upon the world through the advent of the "one who was to come" (5:14), and who brings justification and life for all humanity.

The universality of sin, says Paul, has been countered by the universality of grace. The correlation between Adam (by whom sin entered the world) and Christ (by whom grace has come) has received considerable attention. It has been suggested that here Paul is indebted to Adam speculation in Hellenistic Judaism,[23] such as that found in Philo or other sources.[24] But it has been argued that ideas presented by Philo at least do not form a background for Paul in this matter,[25] and W. D. Davies has suggested that the concept of Christ as a "second Adam" (or "last Adam," 1 Cor. 15:45–59) was introduced to the church by Paul himself.[26] Whatever influences have exerted themselves,[27] Christ is not portrayed here as an Adam redivivus: "Adam and Christ are commensurable, not in terms of nature, but solely in terms of function; the world is changed by both."[28] The attention given to Adam by Paul is not related to the creation accounts in Genesis 1 and 2, as in the usual Adam speculations, but to Genesis 3 (the fall).[29]

In 5:12–14 Paul speaks of sin, death, the law, and accountability. Sin came into the world through Adam,[30] and "death through sin" (5:12). Sin entered when Adam disobeyed the commandment of God (Gen. 2:16–17; 3:3) and thereby sought to be "as God" (Gen. 3:5). The overt act of Adam against God's commandment can be called a "transgression" (*parabasis*, Rom. 5:14), "trespass" (*paraptōma*, 5:15–18), and "disobedience" (*parakoē*, 5:19). But at a deeper level, and at the outset, Paul speaks rather of "sin" (*hamartia*, 5:12). There is a subtle distinction made between "sin" and "transgression" in this section.[31] As summarized by C. K. Barrett, "Sin is an inward disposition of rebellion against God arising out of exaltation of the self. . . . Sin is turned into transgression, and becomes visible and assessable, only when a law is given."[32] Thus sin entered the world through Adam's rebellion, and it can be spoken of as "transgression" in consequence of Adam's overstepping of the commandment of God (Rom. 5:14).

The era between Adam and Moses is spoken of as a time "before the law was given" (5:13). Therefore it was not a time, strictly speaking, of "transgression," "for sin is not counted where there is no law" (5:13).[33] Nevertheless, it was a time in which "all people sinned" (5:12), a time of rebellion against God on the part of all humanity. Consequently, as in the case of Adam, upon whom the sentence of death was pronounced (Gen. 3:19), the sentence of death has been pronounced upon all humanity: "death spread to all persons because all persons sinned" (5:12).[34] The thinking here is that "death comes to man as something for which he was *not* made, as an offence, cutting short and reducing to meaninglessness all that is highest and distinctive about him, the negation of love and his personal existence and values."[35]

In 5:15–21 there is a shift. While in 5:12–14 the solidarity of all humankind as rebellious like Adam is affirmed, so that "death reigned" (5:14) and exercised its rule over all, in 5:15–21 the "trespass" of Adam becomes itself the factor that leads to condemnation of all.[36] The focus is now no longer upon the sinfulness of humanity as such, but upon the effects of Adam's trespass. Now Adam is positioned as the head of humanity. Here Adam becomes much more a symbol, a mythological figure, who symbolizes not only rebellion against God (as one who "sins") but whose "trespass" brought death and condemnation to the whole human race (5:15–16).

The theological shift can be detected, moreover, in the terminology used. In 5:14 Paul had spoken of Adam's "transgression" (*parabasis*). But in the following verses he speaks of the "trespass" (*paraptōma*) of Adam (5:15, 17, 18). A distinction can be made. The former term (*parabasis*, "transgression") implies transgression of a commandment, and Adam's "transgression" of a commandment is portrayed in Genesis. But the latter term (*paraptōma*, "trespass") is a more radical term, an equivalent to "sin" (*hamartia*), the disruption of humanity's relationship to God.[37] Etymologically the word is derived from the verb "to fall" (*piptō*). That the term is equivalent to sin for Paul can be seen through a comparison of 5:13 ("*sin* is not counted where there is no law") and 5:20 ("the law came in to increase the *trespass*; but where *sin* increased, grace abounded all the more").

For Paul, then, "sin" entered the world through Adam, the disobedient one, and all persons have "sinned" ever since. That is Paul's teaching in 5:12–14. But there is more. Adam's "trespass" — his fall — has set the whole world into rebellion against God. All of humanity bears the character of Adam as the fallen one. Paul does not think in terms of a biological descent of "original sin" from Adam to successive generations, as in the manner of subsequent theology, but he thinks of Adam as the prototype or head of humanity in its actual character. So he can write that "by one man's trespass, many died" (5:15). The sentence of death upon Adam (Gen. 3:19) has been extended to all.

Paul proceeds to declare, however, that the effects of Christ's obedience are far greater for humankind than the effects of Adam's fall. Although the contrasts between Adam and Christ are not uniformly developed in exact parallelism throughout 5:12–21,[38] the contrasts are spelled out explicitly in parallel in 5:18–19, as can be seen through the use of parallel columns (author's translation):

5:18

as through one's (Adam's) trespass [there has been] for all persons condemnation,	so through one's (Christ's) act of righteousness [there is] for all persons justification resulting in life.

5:19

as through one's (Adam's) disobedience many were made sinners,	so through one's (Christ's) obedience many will be made righteous.

The contrasts are between Adam's "trespass" (*paraptōma*) or "disobedience" (*parakoē*) and Christ's "act of righteousness" (*dikaiōma*) or "obedience" (*hypakoē*). Contrasts are also to be seen in the results of the work of each. Adam's trespass or disobedience has brought condemnation (*katakrima*, 5:18); through his act many were made sinners (5:19). Christ's "act of righteousness" results in "justification of life" (*dikaiōsis zōēs*) for all (5:18). The term *dikaiōsis* can be translated as "justification" (RSV, "acquittal," but cf. Rom. 4:25 where the same term is translated "justification") — the opposite of "condemnation."[39] The word *zōēs* ("of life") is a genitive of result, providing the outcome of justification, so that the phrase may be rendered "justification resulting in life."[40]

Clearly the universality of grace in Christ is shown to surpass the universality of sin. Christ's "act of righteousness" is the opposite of Adam's "trespass" and equivalent to Christ's "obedience," which was fulfilled in his obedience unto death (Phil. 2:8).[41] The results of Christ's righteous action and obedience are "justfication resulting in life for all persons" (*eis pantas anthrōpous*, 5:18) and "righteousness" for "many" (5:19). The term "many" in 5:19 is equivalent to "all persons" for four reasons: (1) the parallel in 5:18 speaks in its favor; (2) even within 5:19 itself, "many were made sinners" obviously applies to all humankind, so "many will be made righteous" applies to all as well; (3) the same parallelism appears in 5:15 at which "many" refers to "all"; and (4) the phrase "for many" is a Semitism which means "for all," as in Isa. 52:13 – 53:12; Mark 10:45; 14:24.[42] The background for Paul's expression is set forth in Deutero-Isaiah where it is said that "the righteous one" (LXX, *dikaios*), the Lord's servant, shall make "many" to be accounted righteous, and he shall bear their sins (LXX, *hamartias*, Isa. 53:11).

It is significant, and even astounding, that justification here is said to be world-embracing. There is nothing said about faith as the grounds for justification, nor about faith's accepting it. To be sure, some interpreters have maintained that faith is assumed to be a condition, usually basing their claim on 5:17, in which Paul says that "those who receive the abundance of grace and the free gift of righteousness" will "reign in life through the one man Jesus Christ." This, it is said, implies that there is a "possibility" for justification and life on the basis of Christ's work, but that faith is the condition for receiving such.[43] But the verse in fact implies no restrictions.[44] Even here Paul writes that the redemptive work of Christ is "much more" in its

effects than the "trespass" of Adam. Death, because of Adam's trespass, "reigned through the one" (*dia tou henos,* 5:17a), and its reign
was of course over all. But "much more" will the recipients of the
"abundance of grace and the free gift of righteousness reign in life
through the one (*dia tou henos,* 5:17b) Jesus Christ." The parallel of
Adam and Christ is maintained. The parallel of reigning, however,
is disjointed. On the one hand, death reigned through Adam; on the
other, recipients of grace will reign in life. Death can indeed be said
to "reign" over humanity (cf. 5:14), but life cannot be said to "reign,"
for it is an eschatological gift.[45] Paul therefore has to replace the
expected subject ("life") of the clause, even though that destroys the
parallelism. He draws on the traditional language that speaks of the
redeemed as reigning in life (*Pss. Sol.* 3:8; 1 Cor. 6:2; Rev. 20:4).[46] The
point Paul makes is that the reign of death is over since it is
superseded by the abundance of grace and the free gift of righteousness streaming forth upon the world through God's act "through the
one Jesus Christ." Paul uses the aorist — "death reigned" (*ebasil-
eusen*) — to speak of an era that is over, just as he does in 5:14 ("death
reigned"), 5:15 ("many died"), and 5:19 ("many were made sinners").
Then he uses the future tense in 5:17b — "shall reign" (*basileusou-
sin*) — to speak of a reign that has not yet been realized but remains
a future expectation.

But are the recipients of grace, who are to reign, persons standing
even outside the circle of believers? Or are believers alone the ones
"who receive the abundance of grace and the free gift of righteousness"? An affirmative reply to the latter runs into difficulties. First,
it overlooks the fact that the past reign of death is over and done with
through the reign of grace (5:21) which has come through Christ.
Second, it overlooks the nuance of the phrase *pollō mallon* in the
main clause, which can be translated "how much more surely."[47]
That is to say, death has had its reign, but if that is the case — and
it is — then how much more surely will reigning take place for the
recipients of grace! The contrast is not between the many who have
been under the reign of death and the few who will reign in life, but
between death's reign — death personified — and the reign of those
who are recipients of grace. Third, in 5:15 Paul speaks of God's grace
and the free gift of grace in Christ as having abounded "for many"

(= for all). That is the obverse side of 5:17, so that "those who receive
the abundance of grace and the free gift of righteousness" are indeed
all persons. As 5:15 speaks of the scope of grace extending to all, so
5:17 speaks of all being under that scope. There is no reason for saying
that 5:17 places limitations on the "many" of 5:15, 19, and the "all"
of 5:18. Paul's concern is to show that a shift of aeons has taken place.
His interest is not primarily anthropological here. A division of the
ages has taken place: death reigned, but now the righteousness of
God has been revealed (3:21) in Christ's atoning death and consequent resurrection, and his act of righteousness leads to justification
resulting in life for all persons (5:18). The scope of divine justifying
grace extends to all humankind,[48] not believers alone. So Karl Barth
has written concerning 5:19: "In the light of this act of obedience
there is no man who is not — in Christ. All are renewed and clothed
with righteousness, all are become a new subject, and are therefore
set at liberty and placed under the affirmation of God."[49]

The extent to which this passage (5:12–21) can be considered the
"essence" of Paul's gospel and theology can of course be debated. Yet
it must be pointed out that the theme of God's saving action toward
the world in Christ appears in several contexts (as already indicated):
in those passages using the *hyper*-formula ("*for* the ungodly," etc.;
Rom. 5:6, 8; 8:32; 1 Cor. 15:3; Gal. 1:4; 2:20; 3:13), in the theme of
reconciliation (Rom. 5:10; 2 Cor. 5:19–20), in Paul's gospel of the salvation of Israel (Rom. 11:26–31), in his gospel of the mercy of God for
all (Rom. 11:32), and in his expectation of the redemption of the
entire creation (Rom. 8:21). Since the death and resurrection of Jesus
Christ, a new age has dawned which is world-embracing in its
effects. The action of God in Christ toward the world, grounded in
God's own love, has canceled the tension between his wrath and his
desire to save; there has been a "negation of the negation"[50] through
God's self-giving love, by which he has reconciled the world to himself.

It is necessary, however, to turn to other passages by Paul. More
abundant are those passages that speak of "justification by faith."
Beyond these, there are passages in Paul's letters that speak of God's
wrath, those that make a distinction between those who are being
saved and those who are perishing, and those that speak of eschatological peril (judgment and condemnation). Can these be reconciled

with the concept (or gospel) of the justification of all persons through the work of God in Christ?

JUSTIFICATION BY FAITH

The gospel of justification by faith is declared explicitly in Paul's letters to the Romans (3:28–30; 5:1; 10:4), Galatians (2:16; 3:8, 24), and Philippians (3:9). The fact that it does not appear explicitly and prominently in the other letters of Paul has led some interpreters to question its assumed centrality in Paul's theology or to ask whether it is contextually determined. In the first instance one can cite the well-known dictum of Albert Schweitzer, who spoke of justification by faith as "a subsidiary crater, which was formed within the rim of the main crater—the mystical doctrine of redemption through the being-in-Christ."[51] In the second instance there have been interpreters who have claimed that the doctrine grew out of polemics with Judaism or Jewish Christianity.[52] Finally, as a variation on the latter, it has been claimed that Paul's doctrine of justification by faith originated in the apostle's reflection on the relationship between Jews and gentiles: how to defend the rights of gentile converts "to be full and genuine heirs to the promises of God to Israel."[53]

Although the place of justification by faith in Paul's theology will continue to be debated, it is manifestly a major theme, and it is not an exaggeration to say that it conveys the essence of Paul's gospel. To make such a claim is not to exclude other themes, such as reconciliation, the preaching of the cross, or being "in Christ" as conveying his gospel as well. But it is questionable whether Paul's theology can get along without the doctrine of justification by faith. Every interpretation of Paul sooner or later has to come to terms with it.

The doctrine is indeed polemical, and it does indeed defend the rights of gentiles to have a place in the community of the new age (an apologetic function). But it cannot be reduced to these functions alone, since it is based on the prior conviction of Paul concerning the saving righteousness of God for all without distinction.[54] The "without distinction" makes it polemical and apologetic, but the prior commitment to the saving "righteousness of God" forces the polemical and apologetical to take shape. It is not likely that Paul himself would have thought that he was simply defending the rights of gentiles by use of the phrase — although frequently he was doing that (cf. Rom. 3:29; Gal. 3:8) — for he insists that both Jews and gentiles are justified by faith (Rom. 3:30; 4:11-12; Gal. 2:15-16) and that the gospel of the righteousness of God is the power of salvation to all who believe, both Jew and Greek (Rom. 1:16). He most certainly includes himself (a Jew) as one who has been justified by faith (Phil. 3:7-9) and as one who is no longer under the law (1 Cor. 9:20). No one will be justified by works of the law (Rom. 3:20; Gal. 2:16; 3:11). As far as we can tell from Paul's letters, he preached only one gospel for Jew and gentile alike. While that gospel gave place for gentiles, Paul did not avoid evangelizing Jews when the opportunity arose (1 Cor. 9:20; Rom. 11:14). He did not compel Jewish believers to cease observing the law (cf. 1 Cor. 7:18; 9:20), but he did not say that their observance is a means of attaining justification (nor has any interpreter claimed that he did). In Christ there is neither Jew nor Greek (Gal. 3:28). The gospel of justification by faith is declared to all. Moreover, it should be observed that Paul links justification with baptism.[55] Both Jews and gentiles were received into the church through baptism (1 Cor. 12:13; Gal. 3:27-28), and in that event — but not necessarily in that event alone — the eschatological justification is bestowed upon the believer (1 Cor. 6:11; Gal. 3:24-28), who is freed from sin (Rom. 6:7) and walks in newness of life (Rom. 6:4).

The context of justification by faith is primarily ecclesial, rather than polemical, and its results are forensic. Within the heritage of Israel the people of God have their identity in "covenantal nomism" — to use the term of E. P. Sanders. That is to say, "one's place in God's plan is established on the basis of the covenant and that the covenant requires as the proper response of man his obedience to its commandments, while providing means of atonement for transgression."[56] Paul emphasizes a totally different concept. According to his gospel, the righteousness of God has been revealed in the death and resurrection of Christ. As indicated previously, the theme of the righteousness of God, and the theme of justification in other contexts (especially Rom. 5:12-21), are essentially theocentric and world-embracing in scope. But the gospel of Paul has to do double duty. Not only must it set forth the righteousness of God through Christ for the world, but it must also take up the question of *who* now — in the era between the resurrection and the Parousia — constitutes the community of the new age, God's temple (2 Cor. 6:16), those called (Rom. 8:30; 9:24), the saints (Rom. 1:7; 1 Cor. 1:2; Phil. 1:1; 4:22, etc.) — and *on what basis* that is so. For Paul the answer is clear. Those who believe in the gospel of the crucified and resurrected Christ are the community of the new age inaugurated by God.

That answer, however, could be given by any number of Christians. There could be no dispute over the claim that those who believe the gospel constitute the eschatological community. The question remained, however, concerning the extent of the basis for membership: whether belief in the gospel must be attended by circumcision and consequent observance of the law even on the part of gentiles. It is clear from Paul's letter to the Galatians that certain persons had forced the issue, claiming that gentile Christians must accept circumcision and observe the law. Paul opposes all such amendments to the gospel. He argues that no one can be justified by observing the law (3:11). Further, he maintains on the basis of scriptural passages that God had promised to justify the gentiles by faith (3:8) and that indeed one is justified by faith apart from works of the law (3:11, 14, 22, 24). Insofar as Paul opposes those who preach a "different gospel" (1:6–7), his doctrine of justification by faith is polemical. But the issue is finally one of identity. The descendants of Abraham are those who, like Abraham, believe the promises of God which have now been confirmed in Jesus as the crucified and resurrected Messiah. The community of believers includes both Jew and gentile (Gal. 3:28; cf. Rom. 3:30; 4:11–12; 10:12; 1 Cor. 1:24; 9:20–21; 12:13).

The doctrine of justification by faith apart from works of the law has usually been understood in forensic and anthropological terms, and that is how it should be understood, provided that the ecclesial context is not lost. The eschatological community has been created by God through the gospel, which is the power unto salvation (Rom. 1:16); whoever belongs to it is already a "new creation" (2 Cor. 5:17). The final salvation of the world — promised in the gospel of the righteousness of God — is realized proleptically in an actual community in history. Those who believe the gospel are justified, sanctified, and saved (1 Cor. 6:11; 1:21; 2 Cor. 2:15). This means then that believers differ from the rest of humanity not because they will be saved and others will be condemned, but rather because they have been ushered into the new age already, which has not yet happened for the rest of humanity. Justification by faith is then both ecclesial (who constitutes the eschatological community?) and forensic (on what basis has this been determined?).

The language of justification is used by Paul then in two contexts: (1) he can speak of the justificatior of humanity through Christ's "act of righteousness" (Rom. 5:18), which is known only through the gospel, and (2) he can speak of the "realized" justification of believers through faith. Both concepts are rooted in the Scriptures of Israel. The first is rooted in the righteousness of God, which is to be manifested in the coming of the Messiah or messianic age (as discussed previously in chapter 2). Justification in this context is theocentric and cosmic in scope. It is sketched out essentially on an apocalyptic model in that it speaks of the "revelation" or "manifestation" of the righteousness of God (Rom. 1:17; 3:21) and is dependent on a view of the succession of ages, so that the grace of God in Christ has exceeded the divine condemnation following the trespass of Adam (Rom. 5:12–21). In this case God's righteousness is effective for all, bringing "justification resulting in life for all" (Rom. 5:18). God will finally certify his saving righteousness in the judgment (following the Parousia) and complete his new creation in the age to come, be everything to everyone (1 Cor. 15:28), and have mercy on all (Rom. 11:32).

The second (justification by faith) is also rooted in the Scriptures of Israel. Here Paul relies chiefly on the story of Abraham and the promise given to him that in him all the nations will be blessed (Gen. 12:3, LXX), a promise accepted by faith apart from circumcision and observing the law (Rom. 4:9–25; Gal. 3:6–18). All those who believe that the promises of God have been confirmed in Jesus become a part of the eschatological community. Paul also relies on the promise of Hab. 2:4, interpreting it to mean that one shall live (gain life in the world to come) on the basis of faith; faith alone justifies (Rom. 1:17; Gal. 3:11): "The person-who-is-*dikaios*-on-the-basis-of-faith shall live (or have life)."[57] Justification in this context is anthropocentric (or anthropological) and personal. It is sketched out essentially on the forensic model.[58] The believer lays claim to the righteousness and

grace of God, freely given, apart from works of the law.[59] The
believer is justified before God; there is no longer any condemnation
(Rom. 8:1); the believer is already a new creation (2 Cor. 5:17) and
belongs to the new age to come.

To claim that Paul speaks of justification in two different, but
related, contexts is a departure from interpretations of Pauline theology heretofore. Yet it is demanded. Traditionally the Pauline doctrine
of justification has been understood under the (narrower) category of
the full phrase "justification by faith." That is understandably the
place at which the Reformers began, since their concerns were centered on the question of one's standing before God. But the fact that
Paul speaks of justification in other contexts without the qualification
"by faith" (e.g., at Rom. 3:23–24; 4:25; 5:9, 12–21; 8:33) indicates that
the theme cannot be exhausted by the doctrine of "justification by
faith." Within the history of doctrine there have been attempts, to be
sure, to discern certain distinctions. Early Protestant dogmaticians,
for example, sometimes made a distinction between the "objective"
work of Christ — which is sufficient and potentially effective for the
salvation of all persons without exception (for God wills all to be
saved and provides for it) — and the "subjective" assent of faith that
appropriates and makes actually effective the benefits of Christ to the
believer.[60] It has also been proposed that one can speak of "objective
justification" (for all humankind) and "subjective justification" (as its
sole means of appropriation).[61] Yet it has been realized that such
orderings of the discussion carry a fatal flaw: "Does God, who has
reconciled the world to Himself by sacrificing His Son, pronounce
an acquittal only when faith first makes it possible for Him
to do so? . . . The so-called objective fact of salvation thus really
forms only something like a common foundation. It represents a basis
on which the so-called subjective fact is only then able to begin the
really decisive action. It almost seems as if God had to be reconciled
anew through faith."[62] All attempts in the history of doctrine and
Pauline studies to distinguish between objective and subjective justification have one thing in common. The topic of justification is
weighed down and exhausted by the question of the individual's
justification before God. But in order to guarantee that justification
by faith is not thought of as an alternative form of justification by

works—in which "by faith" is still a human achievement—it has to
be insisted that God's justifying grace is prior to faith; faith is merely
the acceptance of it. While that distinction is of course necessary, and
certainly Pauline as far as it goes, in a discussion of justification by
faith, nevertheless justification remains a potentiality, not an actuality, for it is contingent upon faith. Such an approach does not come
to terms with the more radical and far-reaching emphases in Paul's
letters concerning the righteousness of God, God's reconciling action,
and God's justification of all humanity—themes that are cosmic in
scope.

The language of justification is used in two senses by Paul and for
two tasks. In connection with his theme of the righteousness of God,
Paul can say that through the obedience of Christ there is justification
and life for all humankind. The world stands no longer under condemnation due to the fall of Adam. But that good news is known only
through the gospel (Rom. 1:16–17). When Paul goes on to speak of
justification by faith, however, he is speaking of the proleptic realization of the echatological gift in history—and against those who
would place conditions on the gospel. Those who believe the good
news of the righteousness of God constitute the nucleus of the
redeemed while living in the present age. The first usage is theocentric and cosmic; the second is anthropocentric, personal, and—to the
extent that it speaks to the question of identity—ecclesial. The first
is based on an apocalyptic model; the second on a forensic one.

JUSTIFICATION AND
ESCHATOLOGICAL PERIL

The question has to be raised whether the preceding discussion can
stand the test of other Pauline passages. It has been maintained that
when Paul speaks of Christ as the one who has reversed the situation
of humanity before God (so that the divine condemnation has been
lifted), he has all humanity in view. Through the divine action carried out in Christ, there is "justification resulting in life for all persons" (Rom. 5:18); "Many (=all) will be made righteous" (Rom. 5:19).
Justification by faith is the realization in history of the eschatological
justified (right-wised) relationship.

But, on the other hand, a whole host of passages in Paul's letters
speak of eschatological peril. Paul can distinguish, for example,

between "those who are being saved" and "those who are perishing" (1 Cor. 1:18; 2 Cor. 2:15). Various interpreters therefore draw distinctions in Paul's theology. According to one proposal, (1) the work of Christ in justifying humanity is potential, available to the person who believes the gospel; (2) the nonhuman cosmos will be redeemed (Rom. 8:19–22); but (3) nonbelievers will be destroyed or perish in the end.[63] Another view is that in the "universalizing" passages (e.g., Rom. 5:18–19; 1 Cor. 15:22) Paul seems "to have been carried away by the force of his analogy [of Adam and Christ] and argued more than he intended."[64]

In order to pursue this issue, it is instructive to review Paul's language concerning eschatological peril. It should be said at the outset that concepts of "hell," "eternal torment," or "eternal destruction" do not appear in his letters.[65] Expressions of eschatological peril that do appear are the following:

Imagery for Eschatological Peril in Paul's Letters

Perishing for
  Those who reject the gospel (1 Cor. 1:18; 2 Cor. 2:15; 4:3–4)
  Gentiles who sin without the law (Rom. 2:12)

Death for
  Those who reject the gospel (2 Cor. 2:16)
  Those living under the law (Rom. 7:5–13)
  Christians who become slaves of sin (Rom. 6:16, 21–23)
  Christians who have worldly grief (2 Cor. 7:10)

Destruction for
  Opponents of the Christian gospel (Phil. 1:28; 3:18–19)
  Persons in false security at the Parousia (1 Thess. 5:3)
  The Christian of weak conscience (1 Cor. 8:7–11)   15:24

Not to Enter the Kingdom of God for
  The immoral, including Christians (1 Cor. 6:9–10; Gal. 5:21)

Wrath, Fury, Tribulation, and Distress for
  People whose hearts are hard and impenitent (Rom. 7:5)
  The factious who obey wickedness (Rom. 2:8)
  Everyone who does evil (Rom. 2:9)

Condemnation — or Judgment as Condemnation for
  Those who trouble the Christian community (Gal. 5:10)
  The world (1 Cor. 11:32)
  Evildoers (Rom. 2:2)
  Those who judge others (Rom. 2:3)
  Those who resist civil authority (Rom. 13:2)
  Christians who profane the Lord's Supper (1 Cor. 11:29, 31)

Some of these images are used by Paul in the sense of a "realized eschatological peril." God's wrath is and has been revealed against ungodliness (Rom. 1:18); it is exercised through civil authorities against the disobedient (Rom. 13:4); and it is upon the opponents of the church (1 Thess. 2:14–16). God's judgment is visited upon the person who participates in the Lord's Supper without discerning the body (1 Cor. 11:29), and the person who eats unclean food apart from sincere faith is condemned (Rom. 14:23).

What is striking about a review of the imagery of eschatological peril in other contexts is that it refers to virtually every category of persons imaginable: those who reject the gospel or oppose the Christian message, the immoral, those under the law, the world, and even Christians. The major distinction that emerges is the kind of eschatological peril to come. Perishing, death, and not entering the kingdom are not modes of divine action, but of human dissipation, and these are essentially the fate of persons who reject the gospel and live under the conditions of sin and the law. Destruction, wrath (etc.), and judgment, however, are the results of divine visitation. These are reserved for those guilty of overt acts of defiance against God or who oppose the Christian gospel and community. These distinctions, however, are tendencies only. Generally one can say that the more violent or defiant actions of humanity are met with severe divine visitation, whereas the more general condition of humanity under sin is that of being lost, perishing, and dying.

Just as some of the eschatological perils listed are possible for Christians, so in other passages the whole matter of judgment by works in Paul is not a respecter of persons. Every person must appear before the judgment seat of God and give an account (Rom. 14:10–12), or before the judgment seat of Christ (2 Cor. 5:10). Paul writes that God will judge each person according to works (Rom. 2:6). The one who keeps the law will be justified (Rom. 2:13). Each person will receive his or her commendation from God (1 Cor. 4:5). One's end corresponds to deeds performed (2 Cor. 11:15), and this includes the Christian. Paul is speaking of Christians when he writes, "For we must all appear before the judgment seat of Christ, so that each one may receive good or evil, according to what he has done in the body" (2 Cor. 5:10). On the other hand, Paul can write that the saints will judge the world and even the angels (1 Cor. 6:2–3).

It is clear that Paul does not provide a clear, systematic dogmatization of the end times and the fate of humanity. It is too facile to say that, for Paul, there is a clear distinction between the saved and the lost, and that one's status of being saved or lost is determined by faith or nonfaith as in a mathematical equation. Even the Christian must face the eschatological perils coming upon the world and judgment by works—according to some of the passages given above.

To illustrate the difficulties in the Pauline texts, the following passages and comments can be placed in series:

(1) "Therefore, since we are justified by faith we have peace with God through our Lord Jesus Christ" (Rom. 5:1), and "there is therefore no condemnation for those who are in Christ Jesus" (Rom. 8:1); the Christian has nothing to fear in the judgment, for the Christian is already justified by faith and exempt from condemnation.

(2) But "we must all appear before the judgment seat of Christ, so that each one may receive good or evil, according to what he has done in the body" (2 Cor. 5:10). Here Paul writes that each person, including the Christian, is judged according to works.

(3) "In Christ God was reconciling the world (kosmos) to himself, not counting their trespasses against them" (2 Cor. 5:19). The entire world is reconciled to God; trespasses are now no longer computed.

(4) But the world (kosmos) is condemned (1 Cor. 11:32).

(5) All humankind is justified through the work of Christ, whether persons know it or not (Rom. 5:18–19).

(6) But all humankind is yet to be judged, and that will be on the basis of works (Rom. 2:6–16).

The data in Paul's letters do not allow an easy formula. Frequently the solution is to say that in Paul believers are/will be saved, and unbelievers are lost; but believers may also be condemned if they do not keep faith unto the end.[66] But this formula comes under the suspicion of attempting a systematic conclusion where none actually exists.

A better approach is to recognize that Paul writes on different levels of discourse in different contexts. These contexts can be explored under two headings: (1) the world, and (2) the Christian community.

1. *The world.* In Rom. 1:18 – 2:16 Paul summons all the world to the divine judgment. The righteousness of God has been revealed in the gospel "through faith for faith" (1:17). Faith apprehends that God's righteousness has been revealed; and faith accepts the righteousness of God (cf. Phil. 3:9). But Paul also goes on to say that the "wrath of God is revealed from heaven against all ungodliness and wickedness of people who by their wickedness suppress the truth" (1:18). Concerning these two verses (1:17-18), Günther Bornkamm has summarized:

> The revelation of this saving "righteousness" of God is an eschatological event that is accomplished in the "Now" of salvation history. To this same hour is bound the revelation of his wrath from heaven over all the unrighteousness of men. Because he lets his "righteousness" be made known, all the "wickedness" of men also comes to light.[67]

Previously, for Paul, God's wrath has been held in check by God's forbearance and patience (Rom. 2:4). But in the event of the cross and resurrection, now the righteousness of God is revealed as well as God's wrath. Through the use of such apocalyptic imagery, Paul conceives of the end of the ages as having come, in which both God's saving righteousness and his condemning wrath are revealed. The time of "forbearance" is over. Now the entire world stands under judgment and grace.

But this understanding is a perception and claim of faith alone. In the past one could have a certain confidence in the flesh (Phil. 3:4), relying upon one's own righteousness for salvation — or so it was thought apart from present revelation — and one could divide up the world into those who are saved and those who are condemned. But now that is no longer possible. God has consigned all to disobedience (Rom. 11:32; cf. 3:9, 20-21). All stand under God's condeming judgment.

To be sure, in Romans 2 Paul is able to speak of final judgment by works (2:6). He even goes on to say that there will be eternal life for those who have sought to do right (both Jews and gentiles) and wrath and fury and tribulation and distress for those who do evil (2:7–10). Yet here Paul is defusing the presumed privileges of Israel,[68] "for God shows no partiality" (2:11). Paul is an apocalyptic preacher who declares that all humanity is under the wrath of God, who will judge the world (cf. Rom. 3:6; 14:10). The apocalyptic terrors have been revealed to faith in the "now" of salvation history, and this will be revealed for all at the Parousia. All human confidence is destroyed. Humanity has no hope except in the grace and righteousness of God.[69]

It is in light of this apocalyptic outlook that Paul's other statements about the eschatological perils for unbelieving humanity can be understood. While in Rom. 1:18 – 2:16 Paul makes a lengthy treatment concerning humanity apart from faith in Christ,[70] the other instances are brief notices at best. Those for whom the word of the cross is folly are perishing (1 Cor. 1:18); those who reject the gospel are headed toward death (2 Cor. 2:16); and those who oppose the Christian community and are enemies of the cross of Christ will be destroyed (Phil. 1:28; 3:18–19). In such instances Paul does not spell out a doctrine concerning the final condition of unbelievers and persons who have not heard the gospel in general. His focus is on those who oppose the gospel and/or the Christian community, not upon humanity as a whole.

But along with such statements there are countervailing claims, and these are in sections of Paul's letters that are not brief notices but extended theological treatments, holding forth a vision of God's righteousness, faithfulness, and grace. In Romans 9 – 11 Paul takes up the question of Israel within the divine purposes. The logic of the passage is that Israel has rejected the gospel – except for a faithful remnant (11:5) – and therefore merits God's condemnation. Israel has been disobedient (10:21), has not obeyed the gospel (10:16), and "as regards the gospel they are enemies of God" (11:28). Yet Paul concludes that "all Israel will be saved" on the basis of God's election and mercy (11:25–31). "For God has consigned all persons to disobedience, that he may have mercy on all" (11:32).

And God's righteous action toward the world is not confined to

Israel alone. Again it is the case that in longer passages — apart from
the brief notices of eschatological peril — Paul speaks of the salvation
of the world, using various metaphors. In Rom. 5:12–21 he maintains
that the condemnation of the world consequent to the fall of Adam
has been overcome through the consequent "act of righteousness" and
"obedience" of Christ. In 1 Cor. 15:20–28 Paul envisions the consummation of all things. His statement that "for as in Adam all die, so
also in Christ shall all be made alive" (15:22) can hardly be interpreted to mean that he has believers alone (those "in Christ") in view
as heirs of life in the age to come. He does not say here that "all in
Christ" shall live, as though "in Christ" modifies "all"; rather, the "in
Christ" is adverbial — the means by which the "all" shall be made
alive.[71] Furthermore, in the verses that follow Paul presents a panorama in which he envisions first the resurrection of believers at the
Parousia (15:23). Then comes "the end" when Christ delivers his kingdom to God the Father — after destroying all cosmic opponents and
even death itself so that all things are in subjection to him
(15:24–27) — that "God may be everything to everyone" (15:28). In 2
Cor. 5:16–21 Paul writes that no one can any longer be considered
from a human point of view. Those "in Christ" are a new creation
(5:17). But the new perspective is based on the prior action of God,
who in Christ "was reconciling the world to himself, not counting
their trespasses against them" (5:19). From that foundational truth
the apostle and other missionaries are "ambassadors for Christ" to
call upon persons everywhere to be reconciled to God. The indicative
concerning God is the basis for the call of the gospel: God has reconciled the world to himself, so that from the divine side of the divine-
human relationship the calculating of trespasses is over; the problem
remaining is for persons to hear the gospel of reconciliation and enter
now into the new creation, which awaits humanity. Finally in the
Philippian hymn (2:6–11) — which is essentially pre-Pauline in terms
of its composition,[72] but is nevertheless employed by Paul — the apostle envisions the consummation of all things when every knee shall
bow and every tongue confess that "Jesus Christ is Lord" to the glory
of God the Father in the eschatological future (2:10–11); no distinction is made between present believers and unbelievers.[73]

The question can rightly be raised whether in such passages as these Paul simply got carried away and affirmed more than he intended. But the same question can be raised concerning his words of eschatological peril. As indicated, the passages on eschatological peril—except for the treatment in Rom. 1:18—2:16, which seeks to destroy personal privileges and to set all humankind before the judgment of God—are relatively brief notices, while those that speak of the ultimate salvation of humankind are more extensive and deliberate. Moreover, they must be taken with utmost seriousness for another reason. Paul lived in a pre-Constantinian world in which few were Christians. He lived at a time in which Christians made up only a very small fraction of the Roman world (surely less than one percent). It is simply astounding that Paul could take on the whole world in his vision of eschatological salvation. If he truly thought that only believers would ultimately be saved—a tiny fraction of the world's population—how could he have written these passages concerning the salvation of Israel, the justification of humanity in Christ, a final consummation when God will be everything to everyone, the reconciliation of the world, and the final acclamation of every tongue that "Jesus Christ is Lord"? But Paul makes his claims in the face of Israel's no to the gospel, in light of massive ignorance of gentiles concerning the gospel, and in the context of an imminent expectation of the Parousia. The fact that he makes such claims must therefore be taken with great seriousness. Paul's eschatological vision is essentially world-embracing in outlook, and this outlook grows out of his gospel of the righteousness of God, by which God has come to save his fallen world. "The creation itself will be set free from its bondage to decay and obtain the glorious liberty of the children of God" (Rom. 8:21). The "creation" of which Paul speaks is not simply the subhuman created world, but the entire creation, including humankind.[74] What distinguishes the "children of God" from the rest of humanity is that they have already entered into the "new creation" that awaits the rest of humanity and the cosmos.

Although Paul's theological outlook is essentially modeled here on apocalyptic, it is at this place that he transcends the apocalyptic tradition. His gospel of the crucified Messiah, through whom God has manifested his righteousness, springs open the tradition. The apocalyptic tradition emphasizes "universalism" (i.e., all people, not only Israel, appear before God for vindication or condemnation) and "individualism" (each person stands alone before God).[75] Furthermore, in the apocalyptic tradition it is generally the case that only a few will be saved (cf. 2 Esd. 7:17, 31, 47, 61; 8:1–3; 9:14; 10:10). But Paul thinks in terms of the salvation of Israel and the nations through the righteousness of God. And rather than the salvation of a few alone, he is able to think in terms of the salvation of the many.

2. *The Christian community*. For Paul, believers are justified apart from the works of the law (Rom. 3:27–30; 10:4; Gal. 2:16; 3:24; Phil. 3:9), have peace with God (Rom. 5:1), do not stand under condemnation (Rom. 8:1), and "shall be saved . . . from the wrath of God" (Rom. 5:9) at the final judgment. The verdict has already been pronounced. Nothing will ever separate the believer from the love of God in Christ (Rom. 8:38–39). No condemning charge shall be brought, for God justifies (Rom. 8:33–34).

Nevertheless, as indicated previously, there are passages in which Paul says that Christians must stand in the judgment before God or Christ, give an account of themselves, and only then receive the results of the divine verdict, based on "what [a person] has done in the body" (2 Cor. 5:10; cf. Rom. 14:10–12; 1 Cor. 4:5). At the Parousia, Christians should be "guiltless" (1 Cor. 1:8), have "hearts unblamable in holiness" (1 Thess. 3:13), and be "sound and blameless" (1 Thess. 5:23). Moreover, Christians can fall back into slavery to sin or live according to the flesh and thereby reap death (Rom. 6:16–23; 8:13), and the person weak in faith can be destroyed (1 Cor. 8:11). Such passages as these call into question the presumed security of those who are in Christ. If even the Christian is to be judged in the final judgment according to works, the gospel of justification by faith begins to pale in significance. Unconditional grace all of a sudden becomes conditioned by the believer's fidelity.[76]

The passages that speak of eschatological peril for Christians, however, must be seen in their contexts. Three of these have to do with the apostolic ministry. First, in 1 Cor. 3:10–15 Paul speaks of his own apostolic ministry — and that of others (3:13) — as subject to testing by fire at the final judgment (3:14). The apostolic work itself may be destroyed ("burned up"), and the person engaged in it will thereby suffer loss, "though he himself will be saved, but only as through fire"

(3:15). The eschatological peril to come is then purging in its effects.[77] Second, in 1 Cor. 4:1–5, which ends with the declaration that "every person will receive his commendation from God" (4:5), Paul is speaking of his stewardship of the gospel (4:1–2) and calls upon the Corinthians to refrain from making judgments concerning this stewardship (4:3).[78] The Lord himself will judge Paul's stewardship at his final coming, when he brings to light things now hidden and the intended purposes of human hearts (4:5). The "commendation" of which Paul speaks has to do with a verdict upon the stewardship of the gospel, not upon himself (or anyone else) as such. Third, the passage concerning judgment before Christ — "so that each one may receive good or evil, according to what he has done in the body" (2 Cor. 5:10) — appears within a long section of 2 Corinthians in which Paul defends his apostleship. He insists that he and his associates ("we" is used throughout) have renounced underhanded ways (4:2), have the treasure of the gospel in earthen vessels (4:7), have suffered greatly (4:8–11), and are indeed perishing bodily (4:16; 5:1–5). He and his associates are "at home in the body" and "away from the Lord" (5:6). It would be better to be "away from the body and at home with the Lord" (5:8). But in either case, "we make it our aim to please him" (5:9). It is on that basis — the aim to please the Lord in faithful apostolic ministry — that Paul writes, "For we must all appear before the judgment seat of Christ, so that each one may receive good or evil, according to what he has done in the body" (5:10). It is the apostolic work "in the body" that is subject to final judgment. Paul's own expectation of course is that he shall "receive good." So he continues, "Therefore, knowing the fear of the Lord, we persuade persons; but what we are is known to God, and I hope it is known also to your conscience" (5:11). Essentially Paul is then defending his apostolic work.[79] The judgment of God to come upon his ministry — though it is God's alone — should be mirrored in the present judgment at Corinth.[80] In none of these passages does Paul spell out a doctrine of "two ways" for the Christian community at the last judgment. Rather, Paul speaks of final judgment on the apostolic ministry of himself and others, and he is confident concerning judgment upon his own ministry (2 Cor. 5:6, 11). The gospel of justification by faith is not itself called into question.

Besides these passages on future judgment concerning his own ministry, however, there are others in which Paul speaks of judgment affecting Christians in general. Surprisingly, however, these do not set forth a robust doctrine of eschatological peril for the Christian on the basis of judgment according to works. In 1 Cor. 11:27-32 Paul takes up the issue of eating and drinking at the Lord's Supper in an "unworthy manner" (11:27). He speaks of judgment by the Lord, and he says that that judgment is exercised upon Christians proleptically in the present. The effect of such judgment is to chasten Christians "in order that (*hina*)" they "may not be condemned" (11:32).[81] Condemnation is therefore not held out as a perilous eschatological prospect but as something that is precluded by judgment in the present. A similar motif appears in 1 Cor. 5:1-5. In this instance Paul has already "pronounced judgment in the name of the Lord Jesus" (5:3-4) upon an immoral person. This person is to be delivered "to Satan for the destruction of the flesh" but precisely "in order that (*hina*) his spirit may be saved on the day of the Lord" (5:5). Judgment in the community is again purgative in its effects;[82] by passing judgment the person is "prepared" for salvation. Finally, one other passage speaks of judgment of Christians. In Rom. 14:1-9 Paul says that no one should pass judgment on the person who is "weak in faith" (14:1). He declares that the Lord will uphold the person so judged (14:4); the person who assumes that he or she is "strong" is to refrain from judgment and from despising the person considered "weak" (14:3-4, 10). In this context Paul's word about God as judge functions to vindicate the person so easily judged to be weak; God is judge. And when Paul then goes on to say that "we shall all stand before the judgment seat of God" (14:10) and "each of us shall give account of himself to God" (14:12), he is not so much presenting a general doctrine of last things, including judgment by works, but is saying that judgmentalism in the community will be exposed and overthrown, for God alone is judge. Therefore Paul picks up again his exhortation against the passing of judgment on one another (14:13).[83]

In addition to these passages that speak of judgment, there are two others that speak of eschatological peril in the sense of not inheriting the kingdom of God (1 Cor. 6:9-10; Gal. 5:21).[84] These appear within paraenetic sections. Significantly, however, they do not set forth a doctrine of judgment by works or judgment of Christians in terms of good or bad conduct. In the first instance Paul lists categories of those who will not inherit the kingdom, using a traditional list of vices.[85] But Paul does not draw the conclusion that the Christians at Corinth are therefore in peril. In fact, he draws the opposite conclusion: "And such were some of you. But you were washed; but you were sanctified; but you were justified in the name of the Lord Jesus Christ and in the Spirit of our God" (6:11). The triple use of the conjunction (*alla*, "but") is particularly effective. As gross as the sins of members of the church at Corinth have been, such persons are nevertheless freed from sin, united to God, and acquitted; and on that basis a new life is open to them.[86] In the second instance — in the letter to the Galatians — Paul has just spoken of the "works of the flesh" (5:19–21a) and continues, "I warn you, as I warned you before, that those who do such things will not inherit the kingdom of God" (5:21b). His exhortation continues with a listing of the "fruits of the Spirit" (5:22–23). The language throughout, in the context of both passages, is that of paraenesis.[87] It is possible of course for the believer to fall back into the ways of immorality or to live according to the flesh. But Paul does not expect that. He exhorts his readers to shun immorality (1 Cor. 6:13, 18) and to walk by the Spirit (Gal. 5:25), and he fully expects that they will do so. Lacking altogether is a doctrine of judgment by works or by any presumed moral perfectionism of those already justified.

Other interpreters have drawn other conclusions. It has been suggested, for example, that Paul teaches "judgment by works and salvation by grace" in the case of Christians, so that correct moral behavior is a condition for remaining in the salvation offered by grace.[88] Or it has been said that Paul expects a final judgment for Christians that can have two outcomes: salvation for the obedient, and wrath for the disobedient; only the Christian who remains obedient to the hope of the gospel will receive the final gift of salvation.[89] Or, again, it is said that redemption has to do only with the initial act of establishing one's status before God (not the final declaration of one's condition), and that final salvation is dependent on continual "participation" in Christ.[90]

But a review of the texts within their contexts does not yield such neat formulas. The Pauline sayings about eschatological peril in the case of Christians fall into three categories: (1) the testing of one's apostolic ministry; (2) the judgment of God or Christ upon community behavior for the sake of "edification of the church through the protection and nurture of the weak, the discipline of the loveless, the reproof of false teachers, and the warning of the vascillating"[91]; and (3) warnings within the larger context of paraenesis. The first two do not hold out the prospect of condemnation, but in fact vindication or purgation on the way of final salvation. The third—the warnings—insist that those who expect to inherit the kingdom are to shun immorality and walk by the Spirit, but it would be going too far to say that Paul provides such warnings on the basis of a doctrine of judgment based on moral conduct. The language is that of paraenesis, not doctrine. That is not to say that the warnings are to be taken as "mere hyperbole" or less seriously than doctrine, for such warnings are the necessary apostolic word for the occasions to which they are spoken. But it is to say that such warnings are not to be lifted to a doctrinal level, as in the instances cited above, whereby final salvation is said to be contingent upon good moral conduct, according to Paul, and that therefore his gospel of justification by faith is called into question. The warnings function to achieve expected results— good moral conduct—rather than to round out a doctrinal system. Even the immoral man spoken of in 1 Cor. 5:1–5 will finally be saved, and those who are abusive at the Lord's Supper will be too (1 Cor. 11:27–32). The word is to be proclaimed to enact judgment against the immoral in the present time precisely that they may be taught repentance and stand before the Lord as those who have crucified the flesh and its passions and desires (Gal. 5:24), have been crucified with Christ (Rom. 6:6), and are dead to sin and alive to God (Rom. 6:11).

The matter has been very well summarized by Nigel M. Watson:

> Paul's warnings of judgment to come are consistently directed at those who are "puffed up," guilty of presumption, living in a state of illusion. One further conclusion, however, can be stated with a fair degree of confidence: . . . Paul does not intend the message of judgment to be his last word to his readers but as the word they need to hear so long as they remain in a state of illusion. His aim is not to induce a state of despair but rather one of penitence leading to chastened hope.[92]

Building further on the insights of Wilfried Joest,[93] Watson goes on to say that it is the nature of preaching and paraenesis to address both despair and false security. When Paul provides warnings, he does not spell out timeless teachings but is actually dealing with persons in their present situation. Preaching does not "teach the whole of dogmatics in every sermon" but delivers what persons need to hear at the moment.[94] (One is reminded here of the preaching of Martin Luther. In the year 1539 he preached a sermon at Wittenberg on moderation, in which he declared that because of their drunkenness his hearers "cannot be saved" and said that this "great sin . . . makes you guilty and excludes you from eternal life."[95] Such assertions are difficult to integrate at a dogmatic level with Luther's theology as a whole, but he must have considered them the necessary word for the occasion, and they are not untypical of his homiletical utterances.) The word of judgment is proclaimed to shake the hearers out of false security, but it is not something final or static. "It is not given in order to keep the church in a state of fear but leads rather to the place where once more, and once again with full confidence, the gospel of assurance in the faithfulness of God can be proclaimed."[96] It is not, then, the case that Paul's theology contains contradictions. The "antithetical moments" of his preaching are addressed to different contexts, leading his hearers along the way in their earthly pilgrimage.[97]

THE ABUNDANCE OF GRACE

The Pauline concepts of justification and eschatological peril cannot be set side by side in a dogmatic system. The theological heritage of the church since Paul has tried to work out a system, and then that system informs the modern reader when the Pauline texts are read. The Pauline texts concerning the justifying work of God in Christ affecting all humanity (Rom. 5:18–19) — as well as statements by Paul on the salvation of Israel (Rom. 11:26) and God's final mercy on all (Rom. 11:32), the final redemption of all creation (Rom. 8:21–23), and God's being at last everything to everyone (1 Cor. 15:28) — are too easily taken to be instances in which Paul became the victim of his own gospel of the abundance of grace. He actually said more than he intended. For of course, the argument runs, justification for Paul is based on faith; only believers will ultimately be saved, provided that they do not turn aside to unbelief and/or immorality. The passages concerning eschatological peril are brought forth, and the conclusion is drawn that unbelieving humanity is lost and so is the person who is weak or vascillating in faith or conduct.

The preceding surveys call such an interpretation of Paul into question. According to Paul's gospel, the righteousness of God has been revealed in the death and resurrection of Jesus Christ for the purpose of saving the fallen world. In the crucified Christ, God has "condemned sin in the flesh" (Rom. 8:3); "one has died for all" (2 Cor. 5:14); God "gave him up for us all" (Rom. 8:32); and "while we were still weak, at the right time Christ died for the ungodly" (Rom. 5:6).

Justification by faith is not, in Paul's theology, the dividing line between the saved and the condemned. It is, rather, a constitutive part of the Pauline gospel. As the gospel of the righteousness of God for all is proclaimed, those who hear this word and accept it — even while living in the old age — enjoy proleptically that which is to come for God's creation. Justification by faith is itself then to be taken within its eschatological context. Those who continue to preach justification by works of the law are not only wrong in principle (for no one will be justified by works of the law; Gal. 2:16; 3:11) but also in their failure to realize that the new age has come. To revert to justification by works of the law is to deny that the righteousness of God has already been manifested in the cross and resurrection of Christ and that that saving righteousness is effective in the present in the life of the believer.[98] If justification is through the law, then Christ died for no purpose (Gal. 2:21), for then one must still "prepare" in this age for the final justification to come in the new age through performing works of the law. But for Paul the believer is already a "new creation" (2 Cor. 5:17). Now, then, "neither circumcision" (and consequent works of the law) "counts for anything, nor uncircumcision, but a new creation" (Gal. 6:15).

Antiphonal to those passages that speak of the scope of Christ's work as effective for all are those concerning eschatological peril. Paul cannot dispense with the concepts of God's wrath and the annihilation of the forces of evil. Even the works of the apostle himself will be judged, and the judgmental attitudes of Christians will be dealt with severely at the last day. In certain contexts Paul can even say that the world will be condemned, the enemies of the cross will be destroyed, and those who reject the gospel will perish and die.

As indicated previously, each of these statements (and more) has to be seen in its context and function within the letters and also within the context of Paul's gospel of the coming salvation of the world. Paul does not work out a system from which one can make deductions leading to (false) security for oneself and guaranteed peril for unbelievers and/or the wicked. As a preacher, Paul holds out both threat and promise. Each is to be taken seriously. To fail to reconcile the two is not a failure of interpretation, for both themes are in Paul. It might be said that Paul himself failed to work out a consistent picture. But if he had been able to work out a system, he would have failed to be true to his own scriptural heritage of the threat and promise of God, the revelation of Christ to him, and the gospel which he had received. He could not dispense with divine wrath. But he was able to claim, nevertheless, that God's wrath is ultimately to be overcome by his mercy.[99] That has happened *already* in the revelation of God's grace in Christ at the turn of the ages even "while we were enemies" (Rom. 5:10) of God. Therefore Paul can set forth the gospel and a vision of the final consummation of all things under God's grace.[100] "God has consigned all persons to disobedience in order that *(hina) he* might have mercy on all" (Rom. 11:32). At this point in his letter to the Romans, Paul becomes a poet—but not any the less a theologian—concerning the depth of the riches, wisdom, and knowledge of God and concludes: "For from him and through him and unto him are all things" (11:36).

Seen in this perspective, one cannot charge Paul with a mechanistic or mechanical view of the redemption of humankind. Salvation cannot be thought of apart from a living faith, in which God is truly God for the believer, and the possibility of perishing (nonsalvation) is real. The saved are those who believe the gospel, and there is a distinction between them and those who are perishing (1 Cor. 1:18). Yet the direction and thrust of Paul's thinking is that ultimately that distinction will pass away through the divine "negation of the negation," which is always unsettling to a piety that seeks to maintain the negation against those who are perishing.[101] Passages that attest the redemption of humanity cannot be attributed to doxological outbursts that exceed what Paul "the theologian" actually intended. It is precisely when Paul is most explicitly "the theologian" (and giving extensive treatment) that he speaks of the salvation of Israel, the justification of humanity, the reconciliation of the world, and the redemption of the creation. It is at these moments too that his notices of eschatological peril are lacking or overcome.

Paul's thinking along these lines would have been rooted in his own experience. He had himself resisted the gospel and had persecuted the church. Yet even in this time of resistance and persecution—as an enemy of the cross—he was confronted by the risen Lord, whose appearance to him was an act of divine grace (Gal. 1:15–16). As a consequence of that appearance of the risen Lord to him, Paul worshiped him as Lord. So it was possible for Paul to envision yet another appearance of the Lord—at the Parousia—when all human defenses will give way, every knee shall bow, and every tongue confess (Rom. 14:11; Phil. 2:10–11), and finally God will be everything to everyone (1 Cor. 15:28).

The consequences of such an outlook for Christian theology in the modern world are beyond the scope of the present study. Paul is only one part of the biblical canon. The doctrine of a final *apokatastasis* (restoration) of all things in Christ has been a subject of controversy in the history of doctrine, having proponents both in ancient times (Origen, Gregory of Nyssa) and in the modern era (J. A. Bengel, F. Schleiermacher, W. Michaelis), but generally it has been rejected (and was even condemned at the Synod of Constantinople in A.D. 543).[102] Yet this doctrine has not always been repudiated entirely. Barth, for example, has written that "even though theological consistency might seem to lead our thoughts and utterances most clearly in this direction, we must not arrogate to ourselves that which can be given and received only as a free gift." On the other hand, he says, "there is no good reason why we should forbid ourselves . . . openness to the possibility that in the reality of God and man in Jesus Christ there is contained much more than we might expect and therefore the supremely unexpected withdrawal of that final threat, i.e., that in the truth of this reality there might be contained the super-abundant promise of the final deliverance of all men." Moreover, he says, the truth of this reality points "plainly in the direction of the work of a truly eternal divine patience and deliverance and therefore of an *apokatastasis* or universal reconciliation." Even if that is not something that can be claimed with certainty, Christians can hope and pray that "in spite of everything which may seem quite conclusively to proclaim the opposite, [God's] compassion should not fail."[103] So also Dietrich Bonhoeffer wrote:

> God goes to every man when sore bestead,
> Feeds body and spirit with his bread;
> For Christians, pagans alike he hangs dead,
> And both alike forgiving.[104]

NOTES

1. The verb appears fifteen times in Romans (2:13; 3:4, 20, 24, 26, 28, 30; 4:2, 5; 5:1, 9; 6:7; 8:30 twice, 33), twice in 1 Corinthians (4:4; 6:11), and eight times in Galatians (2:16 three times, 17; 3:8, 11, 24; 5:4).

2. The noun appears in Romans twice (4:25; 5:18).

3. These instances are in Rom. 4:3, 5, 6, 9, 11 twice, 13, 22; 5:17, 21; 9:30 twice; 10:4, 6, 10; 2 Cor. 5:21; Gal. 2:21; 3:6, 21; Phil. 1:11; 3:9.

4. The verb is used eight times in Romans (5:9, 10; 8:24; 9:27; 10:9, 13; 11:14, 26), nine times in 1 Corinthians (1:18, 21; 3:15; 5:5; 7:16 twice; 9:22; 10:33; 15:2), and once each in 2 Corinthians (2:15) and 1 Thessalonians (2:16).

5. The noun is used five times in Romans (1:16; 10:1, 10; 11:11; 13:11), four times in 2 Corinthians (1:16; 6:2 twice; 7:10), three times in Philippians (1:19, 28; 2:12), and twice in 1 Thessalonians (5:8, 9).

6. The verb appears twice in Romans (5:10 twice) and three times in 2 Corinthians (5:18, 19, 20). At 1 Cor. 7:11 the term is used in the sense of reconciliation of spouses.

7. The noun appears twice in Romans (5:11; 11:15) and twice in 2 Corinthians (5:18, 19).

8. Both instances are in Galatians (3:13; 4:5).

9. The noun appears twice in Romans (3:24; 8:23) and once in 1 Corinthians (1:30).

10. The question has been posed previously, but it has not received sufficient attention. The issue was raised, for example, in 1963 at the Fourth Assembly of the Lutheran World Federation at Helsinki. See *Justification Today* (Geneva: Lutheran World Federation, 1965), 1–2: "The question was asked . . . whether we may say simply that God justifies the godless without a reference to faith such as Paul makes in Romans 4:5," and Jesus' fellowship

with sinners is cited. The answer was worked out by reference to the Prodigal Son. "Does not this parable say that being received again into the father's house and returning home, that being forgiven and changing one's life, that justification and faith are in actuality inseparable?" In all candor it must be said that the issue was not given adequate treatment by such a tour de force.

11. Cf. Leonhard Goppelt, *Theology of the New Testament* (Grand Rapids: Wm. B. Eerdmans, 1981–82), 2:136.

12. Cf. ibid., 2:137; Victor Paul Furnish, *Theology and Ethics in Paul* (Nashville: Abingdon Press, 1968), 149.; Günther Bornkamm, *Paul* (New York: Harper & Row, 1971), 141; F. F. Bruce, *1 and 2 Corinthians*, NCB (London: Oliphants, 1971), 209–10; C. K. Barrett, *A Commentary on the Second Epistle to the Corinthians*, HNTC (New York: Harper & Row, 1973), 175–77; Harold H. Ditmanson, *Grace and Experience in Theology* (Minneapolis: Augsburg Pub. House, 1977), 193–202; John Reumann, "Reconciliation," in *IDBSup*, 728–29; Ralph P. Martin, *Reconcilation: A Study of Paul's Theology* (Atlanta: John Knox Press, 1981), 32–37; Joseph A. Fitzmyer, "Reconciliation in Pauline Theology," in *To Advance the Gospel: New Testament Studies* (New York: Crossroad, 1981), 162–85; and Margaret E. Thrall, "2 Corinthians 5:18–21: Reconciliation with God," *ExpTim* 93 (1982):227–32. The two concepts have also been linked subsequently, as in the *Apology to the Augsburg Confession* 4.86 and 97; see *The Book of Concord*, ed. Theodore G. Tappert (Philadelphia: Fortress Press, 1959), 119, 121.

13. Cf. also Rom. 14:15 ("one for whom Christ died") and 1 Cor. 1:13 ("was Paul crucified for you?"). For a discussion of these and the texts cited above (all using the *hyper* formula), see Werner Kramer, *Christ, Lord, Son of God* SBT 50 (Naperville: Alec R. Allenson, 1966), 26–28.

14. That the term "creation" includes humanity in Rom. 8:19–23, see Otto Michel, *Der Brief an die Römer* 11th ed., MeyerK 4 (Göttingen: Vandenhoeck & Ruprecht, 1957), 172–73; F. F. Bruce, *The Epistle of Paul to the Romans*, TNTC (London: Tyndale Press, 1963), 173; Ethelbert Stauffer, *New Testament Theology* (London: SCM Press, 1955), 74–75; W. David Stacey, "Paul's Certainties: II. God's Purpose in Creation—Romans viii.22–23," *ExpTim* 69 (1957–58):178–181; John G. Gibbs, *Creation and Redemption: A Study in Pauline Theology*, NovTSup 26 (Leiden: E. J. Brill, 1971), 39–42; John G. Gager, "Functional Diversity in Paul's Use of End-Time Language," *JBL* 89 (1970):327–30; Ernst Käsemann, *Commentary on Romans* (Grand Rapids: Wm. B. Eerdmans, 1980), 232–33; and Ulrich Wilckens, *Der Brief an die Römer*, EKKNT 6 (Köln: Benzinger; Neukirchen-Vluyn: Neukirchener, 1978–82), 2:157–58. The theme of cosmic redemption in Paul has also been explicated by Gustaf Aulén, *Christus Victor* (London: SPCK, 1931), 77–89.

15. Cf. Reginald H. Fuller, *The Foundations of New Testament Christology* (New York: Charles Scribner's Sons, 1965), 204–14.

16. Cf. Ernst Lohmeyer, *Der Brief an die Philipper*, 9th ed., MeyerK 9

(Göttingen: Vandenhoeck & Ruprecht, 1953), 97; Ernst Käsemann, "Kritische Analyse von Phil. 2,5–11," *Exegetische Versuche*, 1:51–95 (esp. pp. 84–88); Dieter Georgi, "Der vorpaulinische Hymnus Phil 2,6–11," in *Zeit und Geschichte*, ed. E. Dinkler, 263–93 (esp. pp. 287–91); and Günther Bornkamm, "On Understanding the Christ-Hymn: Philippians 2.6–11," in *Early Christian Experience* (New York: Harper & Row, 1969), 112–22.

17. Cf. D. Georgi, "Der vorpaulinische Hymnus Phil 2, 6–11," 289–91.

18. Paul does not mean here that the salvation of Israel depends on the conversion of Jews individually or collectively in history. On this matter, see C. K. Barrett, *A Commentary on the Epistle to the Romans*, HNTC (New York: Harper & Brothers, 1957), 227; John Murray, *The Epistle to the Romans* (Grand Rapids: Wm. B. Eerdmans, 1959–65), 2:98–100; Bruce, *Romans*, 223; Oscar Cullmann, *Salvation in History* (New York: Harper & Row, 1967), 162; Bornkamm, *Paul*, 151; Ulrich Luz, *Das Geschichtsverständnis des Paulus*, BEvT 49 (Munich: Kaiser, 1968), 286–300; Käsemann, *Romans*, 314; Krister Stendahl, *Paul Among Jews and Gentiles* (Philadelphia: Fortress Press, 1976), 4; Nils Dahl, "The Future of Israel," in *Studies in Paul*, 153–58; C. E. B. Cranfield, *A Critical and Exegetical Commentary on the Epistle to the Romans*, ICC (Edinburgh: T. & T. Clark, 1975–79), 577; W. D. Davies, "Paul and the People of Israel," in *Jewish and Pauline Studies*, 139–43; and Wilckens, *Römer*, 2:254–56. For an essay that dissents in favor of the view that Paul envisions the conversion of Israel and faith (but that is not clear whether this is expected in history or eschatologically), see Ferdinand Hahn, "Zum Verständnis von Römer 11.26a: . . . 'und so wird ganz Israel gerettet werden,'" *Paul and Paulinism*, ed. M. D. Hooker and S. G. Wilson (London: SPCK, 1982), 221–36 (with English summary). The claim that for Paul the salvation of Isarel is dependent on faith in Christ at history's end is defended by E. P. Sanders, *Paul, the Law, and the Jewish People* (Philadelphia: Fortress Press, 1983), 192–98.

19. So Käsemann, *Romans*, 156, writes that the goal of the argument (in Rom. 5:12–21) is justification.

20. Anders Nygren, *Commentary on Romans* (Philadelphia: Fortress Press, 1949), 20, speaks of Rom. 5:12–21 as "the high point of the epistle." That may or may not be the case, but he rightly sees the passage as crucial to the letter.

21. The phrase is used also at Rom. 4:16; 2 Cor. 13:10; and Philemon 15.

22. Cf. Rudolf Bultmann, "Adam and Christ According to Romans 5," in *Current Issues in New Testament Interpretation*, ed. William Klassen and Graydon F. Snyder (New York: Harper & Brothers, 1962), 153; Barrett, *Romans*, 110; Robin Scroggs, *The Last Adam: A Study in Pauline Anthropology* (Philadelphia: Fortress Press, 1966), 77; Käsemann, *Romans*, 141, 146; and Nils Dahl, "The Missionary Theology in the Epistle to the Romans," in *Studies in Paul*, 90–91. On the other hand, the phrase is said to make a connection with Romans 5:1–11 by William Sanday and Arthur C. Headlam, *A*

Critical and Exegetical Commentary on the Epistle to the Romans, 5th ed., ICC (Edinburgh: T. & T. Clark, 1902), 131; Michel, *Römer*, 121; J. Gibbs, *Creation and Redemption*, 48; and Cranfield, *Romans*, 271.

23. W. L. Knox, *St. Paul and the Church of Jerusalem* (Cambridge: Cambridge Univ. Press, 1925), 133–36.

24. Philo's interpretation of Genesis 1—3 is summarized by Scroggs, *The Last Adam*, 115–22.

25. Cf. ibid., 115–22; W. D. Davies, *Paul and Rabbinic Judaism: Some Rabbinic Elements in Pauline Theology*, 4th ed. (Philadelphia: Fortress Press, 1980), 36–57; and Wilckens, *Römer*, 1:308–10.

26. Davies, *Paul and Rabbinic Judaism*, 44. Wilckens, *Römer*, 1:314, also speaks of Rom. 5:12–21 as "the work of originally Pauline reflection" (translation mine).

27. Extensive treatment and review is provided by Egon Brandenburger, *Adam und Christus: Exegetisch-religionsgeschichtliche Untersuchung zu Röm. 5:12-21 (1 Kor. 15)*, WMANT 7 (Neukirchen: Neukirchener, 1962), 68–157. A brief review is also found in Gibbs, *Creation and Redemption*, 53–56. A fresh approach — that Paul attributes to Christ the role traditionally assigned to Israel in being God's true humanity— is proposed by N. T. Wright, "Adam in Pauline Christology," *Society of Biblical Literature 1983 Seminar Papers*, ed. Kent H. Richards (Chico, Calif.: Scholars Press, 1983), 359–89.

28. Käsemann, *Romans*, 144.

29. Wilckens, *Römer*, 1:310–11; David M. Stanley, "Paul's Interest in the Early Chapters of Genesis," in *Studiorum Paulinorum Congressus Internationalis*, 1:248.

30. The concept is found in Jewish literature prior to Paul e.g., in Wisd. of Sol. 2:24; 2 Esd. 3:21–26; 7:48; *Apoc. Bar.* 23:4; 54:15.

31. Cf. Wilckens, *Römer*, 1:317. On the other hand, Rudolf Bultmann, *Theology of the New Testament* (New York: Charles Scribner's Sons, 1951–55), 1:252, finds the distinction unintelligible. Cf. also his essay, "Adam and Christ According to Romans 5," 153–54, and Sanders, *Paul, the Law, and the Jewish People*, 35–36.

32. Barrett, *Romans*, 112.

33. Cf. Eberhard Jüngel, "Das Gesetz zwischen Adam und Christus: Eine theologische Studie zu Röm. 5.12-21," *ZTK* 60 (1963):54–55: the function of the law is to qualify "sin" as "transgression." Cf. also Gerhard Friedrich, "*Hamartia ouk Ellogeitai*, Rom. 5,13," *TLZ* 77 (1952):527–28.

34. That the Greek *eph hō* is equivalent to "because," see BAGD, 287; BDF, 123 (#235); Bultmann, "Adam and Christ According to Romans 5," 153; Michel, *Römer*, 122; Käsemann, *Romans*, 147–48; and Wilckens, *Römer*, 1:316. Another interpretation is offered by Cranfield, *Romans*, 274–79, who surveys various positions.

35. John A. T. Robinson, *Wrestling with Romans* (Philadelphia: Westminster Press, 1979), 63.

36. Käsemann, *Romans*, 153; Wilckens, *Römer*, 1:322–23.

37. W. Michaelis, "*Piptō*," *TDNT*, 6:172; Cranfield, *Romans*, 284.

38. For example, in 5:12–14 the attention is almost solely on Adam, sin, and death; Christ is alluded to only in 5:14.

39. Cf. G. Schrenk, "*Dikaiōsis*," *TDNT*, 2:223–24; Wilckens, *Römer*, 1:326.

40. Cranfield, *Romans*, 269, 289; cf. BAGD, 198. The construction has also been variously called an "epexegetical genitive" or "genitive of purpose." See Käsemann, *Romans*, 155; Wilckens, *Römer*, 1:326; and Brandenburger, *Adam und Christus*, 233. The meaning is the same in each instance: justification which brings life.

41. Cf. G. Schrenk, "*Dikaiōma*," *TDNT*, 2:221–22; J. Knox, *Romans, IB*, 9:468; Dahl, "The Missionary Theology in the Epistle to the Romans," in *Studies in Paul*, 90; and Wilckens, *Römer*, 1:326.

42. Joachim Jeremias, "*Polloi*," *TDNT*, 6:536–45 (esp. pp. 540–43): Paul "ascribes the greatest conceivable breadth to *hoi polloi*; Christ's obedience affects mankind in the same way as does Adam's disobedience" (p. 542). Cf. also Michel, *Römer*, 123; and Brandenburger, *Adam und Christus*, 221.

43. Bultmann, "Adam and Christ According to Romans 5," 158; idem, *Theology of the New Testament*, 1:302–303. Cf. also Hans Conzelmann, *An Outline of the Theology of the New Testament* (New York: Harper & Row, 1969), 207–208; and Brandenburger, *Adam und Christus*, 230, 242–43.

44. Käsemann, *Romans*, 155; Cranfield, *Romans*, 290, 830. Cf. also Karl Barth, *Christ and Adam: Man and Humanity in Romans 5* (New York: Collier, 1962), 70–71.

45. Michel, *Römer*, 125.

46. A similar switch in subjects is found in 5:15; in the protasis Paul writes "if many died," and in the apodosis, "much more have the grace of God . . . abounded for many."

47. BAGD, 489.

48. Commentators who take this position—rather than speaking of mere potentiality of grace, effective for believers alone—include Adolf Schlatter, *Gottes Gerechtigkeit: Ein Kommentar zum Römerbrief*, 2d ed. (Stuttgart: Calwer, 1952), 192; Barth, *Christ and Adam*, 109–17; Michel, *Römer*, 126; Charles H. Dodd, *The Epistle of Paul to the Romans*, MNTC (New York: Harper & Brothers, 1932), 116–17; Barrett, *Romans*, 117; Nils A. Dahl, "Two Notes on Romans 5," *ST* 5 (1951): 42–48; Käsemann, *Romans*, 155–57; Cranfield, *Romans*, 290, 830; and Wilckens, *Römer*, 1:325–28.

49. Barth, *Romans*, 182.

50. Wilckens, *Römer*, 1:333.

51. Albert Schweitzer, *The Mysticism of Paul the Apostle* (New York: Seabury Press, 1968), 225.

52. William Wrede, *Paul* (Boston: American Unitarian Association, 1908), 122–23; Davies, *Paul and Rabbinic Judaism*, 222.

53. Stendahl, *Paul Among Jews and Gentiles*, 2; cf. 26–27.

54. Cf. Käsemann, *Romans*, 27, who agrees that justification by faith is a part of Paul's "polemical teaching" but also says that it is (as such) "constitutive of the gospel." Cf. also Bornkamm, *Paul*, 13–36; Dahl, "The Doctrine of Justification: Its Social Function and Implications," in *Studies in Paul*, 110; and John Reumann, *"Righteousness" in the New Testament: "Justification" in the United States Lutheran–Roman Catholic Dialogue* (Philadelphia: Fortress Press, 1982), 42, 49, 105.

55. Cf. Rudolf Schnackenburg, *Baptism in the Thought of St. Paul* (Oxford: Basil Blackwell & Mott, 1964), 121–27; Joachim Jeremias, *The Central Message of the New Testament* (Philadelphia: Fortress Press, 1981), 59–60.

56. E. P. Sanders, *Paul and Palestinian Judaism: A Comparison of Patterns of Religion* (Philadelphia: Fortress Press, 1977), 75.

57. So Rom. 1:17 and Gal. 3:11 can be translated; see Reumann, *"Righteousness" in the New Testament*, 57.

58. Ibid., 57. Cf. also Nygren, *Romans*, 81–92; Édouard Tobac, *Le Problème de la Justification dans Saint Paul* (Gembloux: J. Duculot, 1941), 196–99; Ernest DeWitt Burton, *A Critical and Exegetical Commentary on the Epistle to the Galatians*, ICC (New York: Charles Scribner's Sons, 1928), 166. For a discussion of Paul's use of Hab. 2:4 in light of the MT and LXX, see Hans Dieter Betz, *Galatians*, Hermeneia (Philadelphia: Fortress Press, 1979), 146–47.

59. Cf. Helmut Koester, *Introduction to the New Testament* (Philadelphia: Fortress Press, 1982), 2:141: "God's revelation had made justification present for all people. Faith is the realization of this presence." For a contemporary treatment of the theme, rooted in Reformation theology, see Gerhard O. Forde, *Justification by Faith – A Matter of Death and Life* (Philadelphia: Fortress Press, 1982), especially pp. 21–38.

60. Cf. Albrecht Ritschl, *The Christian Doctrine of Justification and Reconciliation* (Edinburgh: T. & T. Clark, 1900), 120–39. Ritschl reviews the discussions of early Lutheran and Reformed dogmaticians.

61. Francis Pieper, *Christian Dogmatics* (St. Louis: Concordia Pub. House, 1950–57), 2:503–12; Hans Küng, *Justification: The Doctrine of Karl Barth and a Catholic Reflection* (Philadelphia: Westminster Press, 1981), 223–35.

62. Wilhelm Dantine, *Justification of the Ungodly* (St. Louis: Concordia Pub. House, 1969), 32–33.

63. C. K. Barrett, *From First Adam to Last* (New York: Charles Scribner's Sons, 1962), 113–19.

64. Sanders, *Paul and Palestinian Judaism*, 473.

65. The concept of "eternal destruction" appears at 2 Thess. 1:9, but that letter is judged to be deutero-Pauline.

66. Cf. Sanders, *Paul and Palestinian Judaism*, 447–53, 515–18.

67. Bornkamm, "The Revelation of God's Wrath (Romans 1–3)," in *Early Christian Experience*, 64.

68. Cf. Barrett, *Romans*, 48; Käsemann, *Romans*, 59–60; Sanders, *Paul and Palestinian Judaism*, 491; Wilckens, *Römer*, 1:127; Ernst Synofzik, *Die Gerichts- und Vergeltungsaussagen bei Paulus*, Göttinger Theologische Arbeiten 8 (Göttingen: Vandenhoeck & Ruprecht, 1977), 80–85.

69. Cf. Jüngel, "Das Gesetz zwischen Adam und Christus," 73; Wilckens, "Exkurs: Das Gericht nach den Werken II (Theologische Interpretation)," in *Römer*, 1:142–46; and C. F. D. Moule, "Punishment and Retribution: An Attempt to Delimit their Scope in New Testament Thought," *SEÅ* 30 (1965):29; reprinted in the author's collected essays, *Essays in New Testament Interpretation* (Cambridge: Cambridge Univ. Press, 1982), 235–49 (reference, pp. 242–43).

70. It has been suggested that in Rom. 1:18 – 2:29 Paul takes over material from his missionary preaching; so Claus Bussmann, *Themen der paulinischen Missionspredigt auf dem Hintergrund der spätjüdisch-hellenistischen Missionsliteratur* (Frankfurt: H. Lang, 1971), 108–22. It has also been suggested that much of it is derived by Paul from a synagogue sermon incorporated and revised by him; so E. P. Sanders, *Paul, the Law, and the Jewish People*, 128–32.

71. That the verse refers to all humanity is affirmed by Albrecht Oepke, "*En*," *TDNT*, 2:542; Jeremias, "*Polloi*," *TDNT*, 6:540–43; Maurice Goguel, "Le caractère, à la fois actuel et futur, du salut dans la théologie paulinienne," in *The Background of the New Testament and Its Eschatology: In Honour of Charles Harold Dodd*, ed. W. D. Davies and D. Daube (Cambridge: Cambridge Univ. Press, 1956), 334; Nils A. Dahl, "Christ, Creation and the Church" in *Background of the New Testament and its Eschatology*, 435–36; M. E. Dahl, *The Resurrection of the Body: A Study of I Corinthians 15*, SBT 36 (London: SCM, 1962), 76, 102–103; and Goppelt, *Theology of the New Testament*, 2:105–106, 132–33. On the other hand, other interpreters claim that the verse applies only to believers: Archibald Robertson and Alfred Plummer, *A Critical and Exegetical Commentary on the First Epistle of St. Paul to the Corinthians*, 2nd ed., ICC (New York: Charles Scribner's Sons, 1911), 353; Clarence T. Craig, *The First Epistle to the Corinthians*, IB, 10:235; Jean Héring, *The First Epistle of Saint Paul to the Corinthians* (London: Epworth Press, 1962), 165; Bultmann, *Theology of the New Testament*, 1:303; Brandenburger, *Adam und Christus*, 72, 140–43, 242–44; Hans Conzelmann, *First Corinthians*, Hermeneia (Philadelphia: Fortress Press, 1975), 268–69 (and n. 49); idem, *An Outline of the Theology of the New Testament*, 187–88; Scroggs, *The Last Adam*, 84; Ridderbos, *Paul*, 341, n. 32, 557–58; and Sanders, *Paul and Palestinian Judaism*, 473. C. K. Barrett has expressed the possibility that the passage may refer to all persons: "The dead in Christ shall rise. This is not a denial that all men may ultimately come

to be in Christ; indeed this may be implied," A *Commentary on the First Epistle to the Corinthians*, HNTC (New York: Harper & Row, 1968), 352. This is a slight shift from his earlier position: "It will not necessarily follow from this that each several man is rightly related to God," *From First Adam to Last*, 73. Early Christian Gnostics understood the passage to refer to those whom Christ regenerates as psychics; on this, see Elaine H. Pagels, "'The Mystery of the Resurrection': A Gnostic Reading of 1 Corinthians 15," *JBL* 93 (1974):284.

72. Cf. Fuller, *The Foundations of New Testament Christology*, 204–14.

73. See above, n. 16.

74. See above, n. 14.

75. P. Vielhauer, "Apocalyptic," *New Testament Apocrypha*, ed. Edgar Hennecke and Wilhelm Schneemelcher (Philadelphia: Westminster Press, 1963–64), 2:590; and Klaus Koch, *The Rediscovery of Apocalyptic*, SBT 2/22 (London: SCM Press, 1972), 30–31.

76. That such is impossible is stated by Paul himself (Rom. 3:3–4) and in the deutero-Pauline 2 Tim. 2:13.

77. Cf. Conzelmann, *First Corinthians*, 76–77; Karl P. Donfried, "Justification and Last Judgment in Paul," *Int* 30 (1976):148–49; Nigel M. Watson, "Justified by Faith; Judged by Works—An Antinomy?" *NTS* 29 (1983):216; and Sanders, *Paul, the Law, and the Jewish People*, 108.

78. Cf. Nils A. Dahl, "Paul and the Church at Corinth According to 1 Corinthians 1:10 – 4:21," in *Christian History and Interpretation*, ed. W. R. Farmer et al., 329–34; Calvin J. Roetzel, *Judgement in the Community: A Study of the Relationship between Eschatology and Ecclesiology in Paul* (Leiden: E. J. Brill, 1972), 167–68; Donfried, "Justification and Last Judgment in Paul," 148–49; Watson, "Justified by Faith; Judged by Works," 217; and Sanders, *Paul, the Law, and the Jewish People*, 108–109.

79. Rudolf Bultmann, *Der zweite Brief an die Korinther*, 10th ed., MeyerK 6 (Göttingen: Vandenhoeck & Ruprecht, 1976), 147.

80. Cf. Roetzel, *Judgement in the Community*, 175; Barrett, *Second Corinthians*, 164.

81. Floyd V. Filson, *St. Paul's Conception of Recompense*, UNT 21 (Leipzig: J. C. Hinrichs, 1931), 86–87; Barrett, *First Corinthians*, 276; Conzelmann, *First Corinthians*, 203; Roetzel, *Judgement in the Community*, 139; and Watson, "Justified by Faith; Judged by Works," 216.

82. Cf. Filson, *St. Paul's Conception of Recompense*, 86; G. W. H. Lampe, "Church Discipline and the Interpretation of the Epistles to the Corinthians," in *Christian History and Interpretaion*, ed. W. R. Farmer et al., 349–53; Barrett, *First Corinthians*, 125–27; Watson, "Justified by Faith; Judged by Works," 216; and Sanders, *Paul, the Law, and the Jewish People*, 109.

83. Cf. Roetzel, *Judgement in the Community*, 134–36; Wilckens, *Römer*, 3:84–86; and Watson, "Justified by Faith; Judged by Works," 215–16.

84. The kingdom of God as future (at the Parousia) in both instances is asserted by Conzelmann, *First Corinthians*, 106; Burton, *Galatians*, 311–12; and Betz, *Galatians*, 285.

85. Conzelmann, *First Corinthians*, 106; cf. also Burton S. Easton, "New Testament Ethical Lists," *JBL* 51 (1932):1–12; and Peter Richardson, "Judgment in Sexual Matters in 1 Corinthians 6:1–11," *NovT* 25 (1983):37–58.

86. Cf. Barrett, *First Corinthians*, 141–42.

87. Cf. Gager, "Functional Diversity in Paul's Use of End-Time Language," 333–36; Betz, *Galatians*, 285; and Sanders, *Paul, the Law, and the Jewish People*, 109.

88. Sanders, *Paul and Palestinian Judaism*, 515–18. But in his subsequent work, Sanders has written that "there is no deed which necessarily leads to the condemnation of a believer," *Paul, the Law, and the Jewish People*, 111.

89. Karl P. Donfried, "Justification and Last Judgment in Paul," 140–52; idem, *The Dynamic Word: New Testament Insights for Contemporary Christians* (San Francisco: Harper & Row, 1981), 57–58.

90. Morna D. Hooker, "Paul and 'Convenantal Nomism,'" in *Paul and Paulinism*, ed. M. D. Hooker and S. G. Wilson, 47–56; cf. also Filson, *St. Paul's Conception of Recompense*, 89.

91. Roetzel, *Judgement in the Community*, 179.

92. Watson, "Justified by Faith; Judged by Works," 216.

93. Wilfried Joest, *Gesetz und Freiheit: Das Problem des Tertius Usus Legis bei Luther und die neutestamentliche Parainese*, 4th ed. (Göttingen: Vandenhoeck & Ruprecht, 1968). As Watson indicates, the book is in large part a New Testament study.

94. Watson, "Justified by Faith; Judged by Works," 218.

95. Luther, "Sermon on Soberness and Moderation, 1539," *Luther's Works* (Philadelphia: Fortress Press; St. Louis: Concordia Pub. House, 1955–76), 51:293.

96. Watson, "Justified by Faith; Judged by Works," 219.

97. Ibid., 220.

98. It is in this sense that Gal. 5:4 ("you have fallen away from grace") is to be taken. "For the Apostle, 'grace' and 'Christ' stand in opposition to 'Law,'" Betz, *Galatians*, 261. The verse speaks of taking up another way of seeking to be justified.

99. Cf. D. E. H. Whiteley, *The Theology of St. Paul*, 97–98, 271–73; John G. Gibbs, "The Cosmic Scope of Redemption According to Paul," *Bib* 56 (1975): 13–29; and F. Mussner, "Heil für alle: Der Grundgedanke des Römerbriefs," *Kairos* 23 (1981):207–14.

100. So A. Oepke, *"Apokatastasis," TDNT*, 1:391–92; and Käsemann, *Romans*, 157, who speaks of "eschatological universalism" in such passages in Paul.

101. So Wilckens, *Römer*, 1:337, writes that "for piety" the "negation of the negation" in God's reconciling work is a "provocation."

102. On the history of the doctrine of *apokatastasis*, see Emil Brunner, *The Christian Doctrine of God, Dogmatics I* (Philadelphia: Westminster Press, 1950), 352–53; Henri Crouzel, "Apocatastasis," in *Sacramentum Mundi*, ed. Karl Rahner (New York: Herder & Herder, 1968), 1:51–52; and Wilhelm Breuning, "Zur Lehre von der Apokatastasis," *Internationale katholische Zeitschrift: Communio* 10 (1981):19–31. According to the *Augsburg Confession*, 17, the doctrine of the Anabaptists "that the devil and condemned men will not suffer eternal pain and torment" is rejected; see *The Book of Concord*, ed. Tappert, 38.

103. Karl Barth, *Church Dogmatics* (Edinburgh: T. & T. Clark, 1936–62), 4/3/1.477–78.

104. Dietrich Bonhoeffer, *Letters and Papers from Prison*, enl. ed. (New York: Macmillan Co., 1971), 349.

5. Paul's Mission

Studies in the theology of Paul do not usually include a consideration of his mission as integral to the rest. His mission is apparently considered his "practical" work, that which he does as a result of his sense of apostleship. But there is another way of looking at the matter. That is to see his mission as integrally related to his identity and thought.

Paul's theology and Paul's mission stand as separate entities when one thinks of his having undergone a "conversion" on the Damascus road, which caused him to reconstruct his theology, and then thinks of his mission as essentially that of having good news to share. But, as interpreters have insisted in recent years, the turning point in Paul's career was not a "conversion" but a "call."[1] The appearance of the risen Christ to witnesses does not in itself lead to apostleship or mission, for the five hundred to whom Christ appeared did not become apostles (1 Cor. 15:6). When Paul speaks of the appearance of Christ to himself, he claims that he was thereby commissioned as an apostle (Gal. 1:15–16);[2] his language appears to be based on the call of Jeremiah (Jer. 1:5). He speaks of himself as called to be an apostle (Rom. 1:1, 5; 1 Cor. 1:1), and so his own apostleship is integral to this thinking. The question has to be raised whether his sense of his own apostleship can be integrated with other themes in his theology.

APOSTLE TO THE
GENTILES OR THE NATIONS?

Paul speaks of himself as "apostle to the *ethnē*" (gentiles/nations, Rom. 11:13; cf. Gal. 2:8–9; Rom. 15:16, 18). As indicated previously (chapter 2), Paul's gospel is essentially a "gentile" gospel in that it proclaims salvation in Christ apart from the law. While he did not draw back from winning Jews (cf. 1 Cor. 9:20), the fact that Paul proclaimed salvation apart from the requirement of circumcision and consequent observance of the law on the part of gentiles means that his gospel had a "gentile principle" and orientation from the outset. Moreover, it was essentially among the gentiles that he carried out his mission.

The term usually translated "gentiles" is the Greek *ethnē* (Hebrew, *gôyim*). As is well known, that term can mean both "gentiles" and "nations," that is, the non-Jewish nations of the world as ethnic, religious, cultural, and frequently political and linguistic entities.[3] Within the letters of Paul it is clear that he uses the term *ethnē* frequently to signify "gentiles" as opposed to Jews (Rom. 2:14; 3:29–30; 1 Cor. 1:23; 2 Cor. 11:26; Gal. 2:12, 14–15). But it is equally clear that the term can also signify in his letter the "nations" of the world outside the people Israel. This is particularly true in quotations from the Old Testament (LXX) at Rom. 2:24; 4:17; 10:19; 15:9b–12; and Gal. 3:8b.

Among the quotations from the Old Testament are references to Gen. 12:3 and 17:5 in which God's promise is made to Abraham that through him the "nations" of the world will be blessed (Rom. 4:17; Gal. 3:8). Paul then makes comments in connection with these quotations, and in each case the term *ethnē* has the connotation of "nations" (Rom. 4:18; Gal. 3:8, 14). Other quotations from the Old Testament speak of the turning of the (gentile) "nations" to God (Rom. 10:19 from Deut. 32:21) and the (gentile) "nations" as rejoicing and praising God (Rom. 15:9b–12 from Ps. 18:49; Deut. 32:43; Ps. 117:1; Isa. 11:10). In the latter instance too Paul appends comments in which the term *ethnē* has the connotations of gentile "nations" (Rom. 15:8–9).

That Paul was an apostle to the gentiles is clear. But it is striking that on at least one occasion when Paul speaks of his mission to the *ethnē*, the sense of the passage is that his mission is to the "nations." Specifically, Paul writes that he has received apostleship "to bring about the obedience of faith . . . among all the nations" (*en pasin tois ethnesin*, Rom. 1:5). In other instances too it becomes clear that Paul's intention was to work among specific "nations" of the world known to him. Although the term is conventionally translated "gentiles" in Gal. 1:16, it most likely has the connotation of "nations." Paul says that he was commissioned to preach Christ "among the nations" *(en tois ethnesin)* and goes on to say specifically that his mission was first to Arabia (1:17) and then to Syria and Cilicia (1:21). In Romans 15 Paul indicates that he had completed his work in the eastern "regions" *(klimasi,* 15:23) and was now planning to travel to Spain via Rome (15:23–28). And in 2 Corinthians he registers his intention to preach the gospel in "lands beyond you" *(hyperekeina hymōn)* rather than working in fields already evangelized by others (10:16).[4]

To put matters rather forthright: If Paul considered himself an apostle to the gentiles, he would not have had to travel beyond Antioch of Syria![5] There would have been enough gentiles in Palestine and Syria alone to consume his energies. The fact of the matter is that Paul traveled as an apostle to the (gentile) "nations" north and west. He intended to go as far as Spain (Rom. 15:28). But as John Knox has written, "it would seem highly improbable either that he would have regarded Spain as a kind of natural or inevitable terminus of his career as an apostle or that he would have given no thought to where he would next go."[6]

When Paul speaks elsewhere (beyond Rom. 1:5 and Gal. 1:16) of his mission to the *ethnē,* the term remains flexible and sometimes ambiguous (Rom. 1:13; 11:11–12, 25; 15:16, 18, 27; Gal. 2:7–10; cf. also Rom. 16:26, which may or may not be genuinely Pauline). If in these instances the term is taken uniformly to mean "gentiles," it can be concluded that Paul went to areas outside of Palestine which were primarily gentile in composition as a matter of course. As apostle to the "gentiles," he goes to the "nations." But such a conclusion is then already conditioned by the dual meaning of the term. As indicated previously, the extent of Paul's travels can hardly be explained by taking *ethnē* to mean "gentiles" alone. The term must have carried with it — in Paul's thought and speech — the sense of "nations" as well, for the evidence from his travels shows that he understood his mission as apostolic work among the various "nations" outside the people ("nation") Israel.

Various passages support such a conclusion. In Galatians the apostle Paul recounts his own version of the apostolic assembly in Jerusa-

lem (A.D. 48 or 49) and its outcome. According to Paul, the apostle
Peter had been entrusted with the "gospel of the circumcision"
(2:7–8) and Paul himself with the "gospel of the uncircumcision"
(2:7); his was an "apostleship . . . unto the *ethnē*" (2:8). It was agreed
that Paul and Barnabas were to go "unto the *ethnē*, and [James,
Cephas, and John] to the circumcision" (2:9). The distinction made
here does not refer to geographical territories explicitly,[7] for Peter
would then have been precluded from traveling far and wide, but
Paul recognized that he did, and that that was proper (Gal. 2:11; 1
Cor. 9:5). Moreover, a geographical distinction would not have been
intended, since Jews ("the circumcision") inhabited various localities
throughout the known world. But it is not satisfactory, on the other
hand, to conclude that the distinction had to do merely with ethnic
(Jew/gentile) distinctions either, for Paul did not conclude that he
could not evangelize Jews at all. Paul did evangelize some (1 Cor.
9:20; Rom. 11:14), and he must have preached in synagogues of the
Diaspora, as Acts attests (9:20; 13:5, 14; 14:1; 17:1–2, 10, 17; 18:4;
19:8).[8] What is more plausible is that the account reflects a general
agreement that the mission of Paul could go ahead unimpeded, just
as that of the Jerusalem apostles would, without rivalry and competi-
tion in each other's field of work.[9] Paul would continue to proclaim
his "gospel of the uncircumcision" (2:7), that is, a gospel that does not
require circumcision and Torah observance. This would be apostolic
work among "gentiles," to be sure, and that is probably its primary
meaning in this instance (cf. 2:12–16), but the overtones of work
among the "nations" of the world is there — not in the sense of mere
geographic entities but in the sense of peoples other than Israel living
in geographical areas composed of various "nations." Paul had
already carried on a mission in Arabia (1:17) and Syria and Cilicia
(1:21). He had been commissioned by the risen Lord to proclaim him
"among the nations" (1:16). Before pursuing this further, the nature
of Paul's call as an apostle needs to be examined in more detail
against its background in Old Testament traditions.

PAUL'S CALL

When Paul describes his call to be an apostle in Gal. 1:15–16, the
language by which he expresses this event is similar to the call of

Jeremiah to be a prophet "to the nations" (Jer. 1:5). Jeremiah cites the "word of the Lord" to himself:

> Before I formed you in the womb I knew you,
>   and before you were born I consecrated you;
> I appointed you a prophet to the nations.

The LXX renders the last line: *prophētēn eis ethnē tethika se.*

Paul says likewise that God, who had "set me apart before I was born," called him for a specific task and revealed his Son to him "in order that I might preach him among the *ethnesin*" (1:16). The latter term is usually translated "gentiles" (RSV, NEB, NAB, and NIV), but it can be translated "nations," and against the Old Testament background this would be its most natural meaning.[10] Moreover, the immediate aftermath of Paul's call was to evangelize the "nations" in Arabia (1:17) and Syria and Cilicia (1:21).

It has been said that, from the postexilic era on, "there is generally a marked dissolution of the concepts of nation and people in Jewish piety, so that references are to the Gentiles rather than the nations."[11] If so, that would mean that Paul, from his Pharisaic heritage, would think of "gentiles" when uttering the word *ethnē*, rather than "nations." Moreover, it is said that conversion to Yahwism was thought of in the era as essentially an individual matter; it is individual "gentiles," not "nations," who (as proselytes) turn from idolatry to serve the Lord.[12]

Yet the matter may not be so simple. Precisely within Old Testament texts that speak eschatologically, it is the "nations" of the world that are in view. Already in Gen. 12:3 the promise (as given in the LXX) is given to Abraham, "in you shall all the families of the earth *(pasai hai phylai tēs gēs)* be blessed." Paul quotes this passage in Gal. 3:8 but alters it to read "in you shall all the nations *(panta ta ethnē)* be blessed." At Gen. 17:5 Abraham is designated "father of many nations" (LXX, *patera pollōn ethnōn*). Paul quotes this passage as well at Rom. 4:17 (as in the LXX).[13] And at Gen. 22:18 the promise is given to Abraham (as given in the LXX), "in your posterity shall all the nations *(panta ta ethnē)* of the earth be blessed." This is alluded to by Paul at Gal. 3:16.[14]

But it is above all in the prophetic writings that the eschatological vision is projected, and these cases envision the conversion of the "nations" to the serving of the God of Israel.[15] Many passages could be cited. Among them are Isa. 2:2–4 ("all the nations" will come to Zion "in the latter days" to learn the ways of the Lord); 12:3 (the Lord's saving deeds are to be made known "among the nations"); 25:6–8 (the Lord will make a feast in Zion and destroy the veil of ignorance spread over "all nations"); 51:4–5 (God's law will go forth, his justice as a "light to the nations," and in his "arm" will "the nations" hope, LXX); 60:3 ("nations shall come to your light"); 66:18 (the Lord will come "to gather all the nations and tongues, and they shall come and see my glory"); Jer. 16:19 (the prophet prays, "to thee shall the nations come from the end of the earth"); Mic. 4:1–3 ("in the latter days" many "nations" will come to Zion to learn the ways of the Lord, as in Isa. 2:2–4); and Zech. 8:20–23 (many "peoples" and "nations" will come to seek the Lord).

Such eschatological expectations of the "nations" as turning to the Lord in the last days are found also in passages within the deutero-canonical (or apocryphal) books of the Old Testament. Among them are Tob. 13:11 (LXX, 13:13, "Many nations will come from afar to the name of the Lord God"); 14:6 ("all the nations will turn to fear the Lord God in truth and will bury their idols"); Wisd. of Sol. 8:14 (the "nations" will be subject to "wisdom"); and Sir. 39:10 ("nations" will declare God's "wisdom"). Still other passages can be found in the pseudepigraphal literature (*Pss. Sol.* 17:30–35; *T. Zeb.* 9:8; *T. Benj.* 9:2; *T. Judah* 24) and in rabbinic literature.[16]

Given the eschatological expectations of his own Jewish heritage, it would be quite natural for Paul to think in terms of the "nations" (not merely "gentiles" as individuals here and there) as the field of his apostolic mission. As J. Munck has written concerning Rom. 15:16–18, Paul thinks in terms of "nations," not simply "gentiles."[17] Insofar as Acts can be used as a source on Paul, the apostle's call is interpreted as a call to the "nations" at 9:15 (Paul is a "chosen instrument" to carry the Lord's name "before the nations and kings and the sons of Israel"); 22:21 ("I will send you far away to the nations"); and 26:20 (Paul preached at Damascus, Jerusalem, throughout the country of Judea, and "to the nations"). This picture of Paul as one appointed to carry on a mission among the "nations" is confirmed by what he says of his work also in Romans 15.

THE OFFERING OF THE NATIONS

In Rom. 15:14–29 Paul speaks of his travel plans but also of his apostleship. Writing from Corinth (ca. A.D. 55/56), he indicates that he plans to travel "to Jerusalem with aid for the saints" (15:25). Paul has completed his collection (Gal. 2:10; 1 Cor. 16:1–3; 2 Cor. 1:16; 8:1 – 9:15) from the gentile churches for the church in Jerusalem. The collection itself was more than a matter of relief, but was also a symbol of unity of his gentile churches with the church in Jerusalem.[18] Twice Paul speaks of his collection as a sign of fellowship (*koinōnia*, 2 Cor. 8:4; 9:13). Paul's plans were to deliver the collection at Jerusalem and then to travel by way of Rome to Spain (Rom. 15:23–24, 28).

Paul speaks of a guiding principle in his apostleship. He says that it is his "ambition to preach the gospel, not where Christ has already been named" (15:20; cf. 2 Cor. 10:15–16). Here he indicates that he will not seek to establish a new "Pauline" congregation in Rome (or anywhere else where a congregation exists) but will go to places where no congregation presently exists. He indicates earlier in the letter that he intends to "impart . . . some spiritual gift to strengthen you" (1:11), and even to preach the gospel at Rome (1:15), but that will be for mutual edification (1:12), not to establish a new congregation in rivalry to the congregation(s) already existing there.[19] He is "satisfied" with the faith and knowledge of the Roman community (15:14; cf. 1:8).

It is in this context that Paul writes that "from Jerusalem and as far round *(kai kyklō mechri)* as Illyricum I have fully preached the gospel of Christ" (15:19) and that he has no longer "any room for work in these regions" of the east (15:23), that is, the regions between Jerusalem and Illyricum. As interpreters have indicated, the geographical references are to be taken not as inclusive of Jerusalem and Illyricum, but as extending between these two poles.[20] Paul has preached the gospel in the geographical arc or portion of a circle — which *kyklō* implies[21] — extending from Jerusalem northwest into Macedonia (which borders on Illyricum). The astounding aspect of Paul's statements here is that, according to him, he has no longer any room for Christian proclamation (and for founding congregations) in the eastern sphere. Certainly he has not preached the gospel to every single person. Certainly there is plenty of room for evangelism among individual gentiles (and Jews) throughout these areas. But Paul says that there is no more room for work in these regions.

The only way to comprehend what Paul has written is that Paul here does not think in terms of individual persons but instead of "nations."[22] Günther Bornkamm has stated the matter well concerning Paul:

> His thought always extends beyond the individual community to countries and districts. Each of the churches founded, but no more than founded, by Paul stands for a whole district: Philippi for Macedonia (Phil. 4:15), Thessalonica for Macedonia and Achaia (1 Thess. 1:7f.), Corinth for Achaia (1 Cor. 16:15; 2 Cor. 1:1), and Ephesus for Asia (Rom. 16:5; 1 Cor. 16:19; 2 Cor. 1:8).[23]

Paul has therefore, in his own estimation, completed the work that he can do in the eastern regions. That does not mean that he has been personally in every nation or province, for he goes on in 15:20 to speak of the labors of others. But given his work and the work of others, he now looks westward toward Spain. It is not likely that Spain would have been the terminus of his apostolic work, but that is where he intended to go when he wrote to the Roman community. John Knox has suggested that the word *kyklō* (15:19) may indicate that Paul intended to go beyond Spain, however. The term implies a complete circle, and perhaps Paul had thus already projected his apostolic work as extending to all the nations around the Mediterranean Sea:

> The gospel preaching in that segment of this circle whose limits are roughly indicated by "from Jerusalem to Illyricum" has been completed; the rest of the circle has to be filled in. It is at least possible that this rather casual *kyklō* reflects Paul's hope and expectation of making a complete circuit of the nations, both north and south of the Sea, planting the gospel where it had not been planted by another. If this should be true, his over-all conception of his apostolic mission would not have been of a series of missionary journeys between Jerusalem and various points in Asia Minor and Greece, but rather of one great journey beginning and ending at Jerusalem, but encompassing the whole Mediterranean world in its scope.[24]

The suggestion of Knox — and he offers it only as a suggestion — deserves attention. Whether Paul thought that he could encircle the

Mediterranean world within his own lifetime cannot be determined with certainty. But the insight of Knox that Paul did not think of his journeys as sporadic, random skirmishes into gentile lands (a point that can be confirmed; cf. 2 Cor. 1:17; 2:12), but as forming a geographic pattern of an arc extending from Jerusalem to Illyricum and then on to Spain, is sound. Paul expected to carry out this mission, although his expectation was finally not fulfilled. It is surely plausible that if Paul had reached Spain, he would have crossed to northern Africa. It has been suggested that his attention would have turned to Gaul and Britain — areas of which he may well have been aware.[25] Yet it is more likely that Paul would have planned to go from Spain to northern Africa. It is there that we have both literary and archaeological evidence of Jewish communities, and Paul would have considered their synagogues as bases of evangelization among the so-called gentile "God-fearers" (see the section below on "Paul's Strategy"). Literary evidence indicates the presence of Jewish communities in Libya (Acts 2:10) and Egypt (Philo, *Legatio ad Gaium*, 36; *Elephantine Papyri*), particularly Alexandria, at which Philo estimated that a million Jews lived (*In Flaccum*, 6.8). Adolf Deissmann has mapped out the existence of 143 Jewish communities outside Palestine encircling the Mediterranean basin, based on archaeological as well as literary evidence, and several of these dot his map across northern Africa.[26]

In any case, Paul's statements in Rom. 15:14–29 indicate that he envisioned his mission to various "nations" extending across a geographic arc. He did not think in terms of individual "gentiles" so much as "nations," planting the church among the nations of the world known to him. Therefore he speaks of his mission as directed toward various countries and geographical regions (Gal. 1:17, 21; Rom. 15:19, 23, 24, 26, 28; 2 Cor. 10:16). And he could write that God always leads him and his associates in triumph and "through us spreads the fragrance of the knowledge of him everywhere" (2 Cor. 2:14), and "grace extends to more and more people" (2 Cor. 4:15).

It is against this background that the difficult verse at Rom. 15:16 can be understood. Paul speaks of himself as a "minister *(leitourgos)* of Christ Jesus to the nations *(eis ta ethnē)*, serving as a priest *(hierourgounta)* of the gospel of God, in order that the offering of the nations (*prosphora tōn ethnōn*) may be acceptable, sanctified by the Holy Spirit." Using cultic language, Paul speaks of himself as serving as a priest making an offering to God.[27] The offering that he presents is the "offering of the nations," which is to be understood not as an offering "from" (subjective genitive) the nations, but the nations themselves—"the offering that consists of the nations."[28]

The imagery recalls that of Sir. 50:12-13, in which the writer describes the cultic activity of Simon as high priest (ca. 219-196 B.C.). In this scene priests from all around (*kyklothen*) surround (*kykloun*) the high priest. Together they present an offering (*prosphora*) before the congregation (Israel) as an act of priestly service (*leitourgoun*) for the Most High, the Almighty (*pantokratōr*).

This cultic imagery lies behind the passage of Rom. 15:16 (that Paul was familiar with Sirach is beyond dispute, since his letters contain allusions to it elsewhere[29]). Paul speaks of himself as carrying out the priestly work of presenting now the gentile nations themselves from the regions of his missionary work extending in the arc (*kyklō*, 15:19) from Jerusalem to Illyricum. The offering is not simply an offering of "the gentiles" (RSV), but the gentile "nations." The phrase "offering of the nations" recalls the closing words of Isaiah 66, which speak of the end times: God will come and "gather all the nations and tongues; and they shall come and shall see my glory" (66:18). God will send his witnesses to declare his glory "among the nations" (66:19). "And they shall bring all your brethren from all the nations as an offering to the Lord" (LXX, *ek pantōn tōn ethnōn dōron kyriō*, 66:20).[30] In spite of the terminological difference of *dōron* ("gift," Isa. 66:20) and *prosphora* ("offering," Rom. 15:16), the concept of the "offering of the nations" to the Lord in Isaiah must be considered the background for the apostle's own expression in Romans, as various interpreters have held.[31] A similar expression appears at Phil. 2:17 where Paul speaks of the faith of the Philippians as an "offering and service," using still other terms (*thusia kai leitourgia*); cf. also 4:18.

The "offering" of which Paul speaks (Rom. 15:16) is presumably not "the Gentile world itself,"[32] for the offering is one that has been "sanctified by the Holy Spirit." That would include Christians alone (cf. 1 Cor. 1:2; 6:11, in which the term "sanctified" applies to Christians).[33] But an offering in Jewish tradition is always representative of the whole. Elsewhere Paul uses the cultic language of "first fruits" (*aparchē*) offered to God to speak of his first converts of Asia (Rom. 16:5) and Achaia (1 Cor. 16:15), and he speaks of Christians generally as those who have the "first fruits" (*aparchē*) of the Spirit" (Rom. 8:23),[34] and on one occasion he speaks of Jewish Christians as "first fruits" (*aparchē*, Rom. 11:16).[35] The church planted is the "first fruits" of the Spirit offered to God (cf. also 2 Thess. 2:15; James 1:18; Rev. 14:4; *1 Clem.* 42:4). In spite of differences in terminology between "offering" (*prosphora*) in Rom. 15:16 and "first fruits" (*aparchē*) elsewhere in Paul's writings, the first can be accounted for by allusion to Sir. 50:13, and the two terms are associated, as witnessed by the fact that later on the writer of the *Apostolic Constitutions* speaks of Christians as "first fruits" (*aparchē*) and "offerings" (*prosphorai*) offered (*prospheromenai*) to God (2.26.2).[36] Already in the Old Testament the term *aparchē* is used beyond the meaning of "first fruits" to include regular offerings brought to the temple or to the priests;[37] the verb "to offer" (*prospherein*) takes "first fruits" (*aparchē*) as its direct object (Lev. 2:12; Num. 5:9); and in Sirach 35 various terms concerning offerings are used in parallel: 35:5, *prosphora;* 35:6, *thusia;* and 35:7, *aparchē*.[38] Furthermore, there is a linkage in terminology even in Paul's own writings in that the "offering" (*prosphora*) is "sanctified by the Holy Spirit" (Rom. 15:16) and Christians as "first fruits" (*aparchē*) are such because of the work of the Spirit in them (Rom. 8:23).

For Paul, then, the "offering of the nations . . . sanctified by the Holy Spirit" (Rom. 15:16) — an offering prepared through his priestly service of the gospel — is the "first fruits" of redeemed humanity. The imagery of "first fruits" is based on the Old Testament cultic festival, by which the first fruits were given to the Lord (Exod. 23:16; 34:26; Num. 28:26; Deut. 26:1-11). Through this act God is acknowledged to be the actual owner of all things; the remaining crop is sanctified, and it therefore shares in the divine blessing;[39] the first fruits "represent the whole."[40] In his apostolic work the apostle Paul intended to gather from the nations an offering acceptable to God — sanctified by the Spirit — by which the divine blessing extends to the nations themselves. For God is the owner of all the nations — the God who is God of both Jews and gentiles (Rom. 3:29). Through his proclamation of

the gospel from Jerusalem to Illyricum, which was to be extended to
Spain and perhaps beyond, Paul made a circuit (15:19) among the
nations to render to the Lord the "offering of the nations" in terms
of the eschatological expectation expressed in Isaiah 66. God leads his
apostle in triumph through the nations and "through us spreads the
fragrance of the knowledge of him everywhere" (2 Cor. 2:14), and
"grace extends to more and more people" (2 Cor. 4:15).

Other passages cohere with this conception. At Rom. 11:25 Paul
writes that a "partial hardening"[41] has come upon Israel "until *to
plērōma tōn ethnōn* comes in." The phrase is difficult, and it has been
translated "the full number of the Gentiles" (RSV). And so it has been
said that here Paul speaks of "the full number of the elect from
among the Gentiles."[42] But such an interpretation tends to individu-
alize. It is not likely that Paul has in mind here a set "number" of elect
persons.[43] Rather, behind the conception is the tradition that comes
to expression in Mark 13:10: "The gospel must first be preached to all
the nations" before the Parousia.[44] Israel's no to the gospel has
provided opportunity for the gospel to be preached to all the nations.
Already in 11:11–12 Paul has written that through the trespass of
Israel — Israel's refusal to accept the gospel — salvation has come to
the nations (*tois ethnesin*), resulting in "riches for the world" and
"riches for the nations" (*ethnōn*). Again it is customary to speak of
"gentiles" in these verses, but Paul thinks in terms of collectives:
Israel, the world, and the nations. Paul envisions the no of Israel to
persist until the Parousia — and then "all Israel will be saved"
(11:26–32) — but that means that in the present time before the Parousia the gospel is to be proclaimed until the "fullness of the (gentile)
nations" enter into the kingdom. Paul does not thereby think that all
gentiles individually throughout the nations will be converted, but
rather that the "fullness of the nations" will be ushered into the kingdom representatively by those who believe throughout the various
nations of the world.[45] The gospel must therefore be preached among
them at the dawn of the new age, which has begun with the resurrection of Jesus from the dead. The eschatological expectation of the Old
Testament that in the latter days the nations will come to worship the
God of Israel is thus being realized — with the apostle himself leading
the procession.

Paul carries on his apostolic work among the nations then in order
to gather from them an "offering" sanctified by the Holy Spirit and
acceptable to God (Rom. 15:16), which is representative of the
nations themselves. This offering is the "first fruits" (Rom. 16:5; 1
Cor. 16:15; cf. Rom. 8:23) of the redeemed humanity. The church is
the eschatological people of God in history, consisting of persons from
all the nations, who are already the "new creation" (2 Cor. 5:17).
That which is in store for all the nations, through God's reconciling
the world to himself in Christ (2 Cor. 5:19), is realized proleptically
in the old age (historical time), where the first fruits appear. Paul's
proclamation of the gospel among the nations is his priestly work to
prepare an acceptable offering, sanctified by the Spirit, as the first
fruits of the new creation.

PAUL'S STRATEGY

There are essentially two competing views concerning Paul's mission strategy. One view, perhaps the most common, is that Paul's work
as an apostle was conducted chiefly, but not exclusively, among the
so-called gentile God-fearers who attended the synagogues of the
Diaspora,[46] that is, gentiles who did not undergo circumcision to
become members of the people of Israel, but who were attracted to
and devoted to Jewish monotheism and ethics.[47] The technical terms
(*sebomenoi ton theon* and *phoboumenoi ton theon*), usually translated "God-fearers," appear in the writings of Josephus (*Ant.* 14.110),
frequently in Acts (10:2, 23, 35; 13:16, 26, 50; 16:14; 17:4, 17),[48] and
in inscriptions.[49] Apart from the technical terms themselves, there is
additional evidence that Jewish communities attracted gentiles who
did not become full proselytes. Josephus writes concerning the Jewish
community at Antioch of Syria: "They were constantly attracting to
their religious ceremonies multitudes of Greeks, and these they had
in some measure incorporated with themselves" (*J.W.* 7.45).[50]

The basis for the view that Paul worked among the God-fearers of
the synagogues rests essentially on the accounts in Acts. Even though
it is recognized that Acts is a secondary source on Paul's mission
activities, it is concluded that on this point Acts is essentially correct.
In Acts, Paul frequently visits synagogues (9:20; 13:5, 14; 14:1; 17:1–2,
10, 17; 18:4, 19; 19:8), and at 17:1–4 and 18:4 it is said explicitly that

Paul found a following from among the God-fearers. For all of its idealization, it is held that Acts reflects rudiments of Paul's strategy.

The second view looks at the evidence from the letters of Paul apart from Acts. When Paul refers to his converts, nowhere does he speak of them as former God-fearers. Instead they are spoken of as having come from pagan backgrounds. The Galatians, he says, had been "in bondage to beings that by nature were no gods" (Gal. 4:8). The Corinthians had been "heathen" and "led astray to dumb idols" (1 Cor. 12:2; cf. 6:9–11). The Thessalonians had "turned to God from idols" (1 Thess. 1:9). Moreover, when Paul speaks of his first contact with the Galatians he says that it was "because of a bodily ailment" (Gal. 4:13). Therefore it has been claimed that when Paul entered a given community, he did not apparently go to the synagogue but sought out and went directly to gentiles.[51] More specifically, it has been suggested that Paul capitalized on his trade as an artisan (tent maker), so that his first contacts in a community were often with fellow artisans and their customers; "that the workshop itself may have been a locus of much of Paul's missionary preaching and teaching is not implausible."[52]

This view sets the material in Acts aside and correctly approaches the matter on the basis of evidence in Paul's own letters. It could, however, be given additional support from Acts. According to Acts 18:1–3, when Paul arrived at Corinth he sought out Aquila and Priscilla "because he was of the same trade" (a tent maker). One could conclude from this that the house of this couple and/or their place of trade, rather than the synagogue, was the locus of Paul's missionary work at Corinth. It corroborates the evidence and inferences from the letters.

But does an either/or choice have to be made between these two views? Immediately after the passage just cited, Luke adds that Paul "argued in the synagogue every sabbath, and persuaded Jews and Greeks" (18:4). Whether Acts can be considered reliable is of course disputed, but to remain for a moment with its account, it has to be said that, according to Luke, Paul did not seek out Aquila and Priscilla simply because they were of the same trade, but primarily because they were Christians, which may well have been known to him through the network of associations within the trade or even simply through information carried about by other Christians who had been in Corinth. They were Jewish Christians who had been expelled from Rome (ca. A.D. 49) when Claudius "commanded all the Jews to leave Rome" (Acts 18:2). Because they were of the same trade, Paul "stayed with them" and "worked" at the same trade (18:3). Their home may well have been the first meeting place for the church at Corinth, just as later their home was the place for the gathering of a church at Ephesus (1 Cor. 16:19; cf. 8:9) and perhaps at Rome after their return there (Rom. 16:3–5), if Romans 16 was directed there. But even though the home of this couple may have served as a place for gathering, according to Luke, Paul carried on evangelistic efforts at the synagogue (Acts 18:4).

The question, of course, is whether any of the material from Acts can be considered reliable on this matter. A case can be made for an affirmative conclusion. In reference to Corinth in particular, it is in correspondence with that church that Paul says that, in his work as an apostle, he "became as a Jew, in order to win Jews" and "became as one outside the law . . . that I might win those outside the law" (1 Cor. 9:20–21). It is in this correspondence also that he speaks of both "Jews and Greeks" as those who have been called (1 Cor. 1:24) and baptized (1 Cor. 12:13). Further, he says that those who are circumcised should not "seek to remove the marks of circumcision" (1 Cor. 7:18), and he says that the Corinthians should give no offense to Jews, Greeks, or the church of God (1 Cor. 10:32). Although the church was undoubtedly composed chiefly of gentiles, it must have had some members of Jewish heritage as well.[53] The data cited gives credence to the tradition in Acts that at Corinth Paul reached both Jews and gentile God-fearers at the synagogue.

Going beyond the Corinthian situation, there are indications here and there in his letters that Paul came into conflict with synagogue authorities and perhaps other adherents. Paul reports that he had received the thirty-nine lashes from the Jews no less than five times (2 Cor. 11:24), and on other occasions he refers to persecutions (2 Cor. 4:9; 12:10), "danger from my own people" (2 Cor. 11:26), and persecution from fellow Jews specifically on the grounds of his preaching (in which he does not preach circumcision, Gal. 5:11). It is through the preaching of Christ, he says, that the "veil" over the minds of those

who hear Moses read (in the synagogue) is removed (2 Cor. 3:14–16).
The conclusion to be drawn is that he had offended synagogue
leaders and was punished by them,[54] and the reason for such offenses
and consequent punishments must have been his preaching in synagogues.

There may be additional support for a Pauline mission to God-
fearers in his letter to the Thessalonians, but this is not certain. At
1 Thess. 2:14 it is said that the Thessalonians suffered persecution
from their "countrymen," and at 2:16 it is said that Jews hinder the
mission to gentiles. The passage (2:13–16) presents a host of problems.
There is considerable doubt whether the passage was actually composed by Paul. Some interpreters consider it to be Pauline,[55] but
others consider it to be a later interpolation.[56] If it was composed by
Paul, it corresponds with data in Acts 17:1–5 where the "countrymen"
are Jews who persecute gentile God-fearers from the synagogue who
follow Paul (17:4).[57] On the other hand, if it is an interpolation, it
may simply reflect the data in Acts, and therefore it may or may not
reflect the actual circumstances of the origins of the church at Thes-
salonica, but in any case it cannot then be evidence from Paul himself. We shall probably have to leave the question open regarding this
particular passage.

The fact that Paul speaks of his converts as persons who had turned
from idolatry to worship God does not negate or undermine the view
that many of his converts were formerly gentile God-fearers. Some of
his gentile converts would undoubtedly have come directly from a
pagan past (without synagogue associations) into his churches (cf. 1
Cor. 6:11, "and such were some of you," referring to many categories,
including idolators). But a good portion of a Pauline congregation
could nevertheless have been made up of God-fearers whose ultimate
origins were in paganism. The God-fearers were customarily first-
generation God-fearers with a pagan past. It was common for such
persons to incorporate the next generation into Judaism through circumcision and baptism; or the second generation would seek full
inclusion on its own initiative.[58] Therefore when Paul speaks about
the pagan past of persons in his congregations (1 Cor. 12:2; Gal. 4:8;
1 Thess. 1:9), we need not conclude that these persons had never had
any associations with synagogues. Their roots may indeed have been

in paganism and their idolatry recent. God-fearers remained legally gentiles, had a loose relationship to the synagogue, and did not cut off associations with the larger pagan environment. They never went through a "conversion," properly speaking, for that could come about only by circumcision and baptism in the case of Judaism. When Paul has to contend with gentile Christians at Corinth for their syncretistic practices (1 Cor. 10:7, 14–22), we witness the difficulty these persons had in breaking with former associations even as baptized Christians.

The view that Paul would not have sought converts from among the God-fearers at synagogues has been given added force by assertions of E. P. Sanders that need to be addressed. Paul considered himself to be an apostle to the gentiles, and in order to win such persons, says Sanders, he would have had to live as a gentile in the communities he entered.[59] Paul's statement in 1 Cor. 9:20–21, in which he says that he "became as a Jew, in order to win Jews" and "became as one outside the law . . . that [he] might win those outside the law," cannot be considered a literal description of his missionary practices. Surely Paul would not be able to carry on in this manner of conduct in the *same* congregation within a given community,[60] and yet it would have been unthinkable for Paul that his converts would comprise two congregations — one of Torah observant Jewish Christians, and another of nonobservant gentile Christians — in a given community.[61] The statement in 1 Cor. 9:20–21 must be considered hyperbolic.[62] Paul conducted himself as a gentile. And the view that he preached in synagogues, and that his converts consisted of Jews, proselytes, and God-fearers must be rejected.[63]

This position is intriguing. But it is encumbered by the fact that it is worked out in argument against another position. It seeks to refute the view that Paul, upon entering a city, went to the synagogue(s) to evangelize Jews, and that when he failed in that, he turned to gentiles. But while arguing against this latter point of view, Sanders seems to go too far, in our view, in portraying Paul as virtually avoiding the synagogues of the communities he entered. It may well be true that he did not go to the synagogues to win Jews, but he could nevertheless have sought primarily to reach gentile God-fearers who were spiritually on the fringe of the synagogues, as well as any Jews and proselytes that might listen to him. That would explain why he suffered punishment from synagogue authorities. It is difficult to imagine that Paul would have been punished and persecuted if he avoided synagogue communities and lived solely as a gentile among gentile populations. Furthermore, the view that 1 Cor. 9:20–21 must be considered hyperbolic because Paul could not be all things to all persons in the same congregation does not follow. Paul does not imply in this passage that he continued to conduct himself as a Jew with Jewish Christians and as a gentile with the rest in the same congregation on a permanent basis. He speaks in these verses, rather, about his initial contacts with Jews and gentiles—persons who had not yet been won—"in order to win" them. But within a given congregation of mixed membership, he insisted that fellowship in Christ breaks down the outer distinctions between Jew and gentile (Gal. 3:28).[64] He recognized, when writing to the Romans, that some believers, on the basis of conscience (Rom. 14:5–6, 14), will continue to observe dietary practices and the sabbath (14:2–3, 5–6) even in mixed situations. He does not dispute this stance, but actually defends those who hold it, saying that there should be no "disputes over opinions" (14:1) nor passing of judgments (14:3–4, 10, 13). All should seek peace and mutual edification (14:19). The implication is that Paul sought to engender respect among all for the rights of all, and at the same time he insisted that through faith and baptism there is a unity which cannot be broken. Although problems would no doubt arise from the competing claims of individual convictions and corporate commitment, no one is exempt from the task of living within that tension, granting rights to the other and seeking to build up the community in love.

Taking the evidence as a whole, it can be concluded that Paul carried on his work as an apostle to the gentiles in various settings, as these gave him opportunity. His work as an artisan provided contacts. His bodily ailment, needing attention, opened up contacts in Galatia, as he says (Gal. 4:13). And the synagogues of the Diaspora were also fertile ground. It was at the synagogues that he would have found gentile God-fearers who were already worshiping the God of Israel and had some acquaintance with the scriptural traditions of Israel. To such persons Paul could proclaim the crucified and risen

Jesus as the Messiah and declare that they need not undergo circumcision and observe the law to be full members of the people of God —
for whom the scriptural promises have been confirmed in Jesus as the
Messiah — but could be full members by faith alone apart from the
law. By going to the synagogues Paul would not have thought of himself as reneging on the agreement at Jerusalem, by which he would
go to the gentiles (Gal. 2:7–10). He would still have thought of his
apostolic mission as directed toward the gentiles among the various
nations. But in terms of strategy, he would find gentile God-fearers
most likely to be prepared and receptive of the gospel. However
schematized and idealized the picture in Acts, it cannot be dismissed
wholesale.[65] Both within the international network of artisans and in
the circle of gentiles already favorably disposed to Judaism (but not
yet full members of Israel), the apostle would most naturally find
access to possible converts.

PAUL'S GOSPEL AND MISSION

The results of this chapter and the previous ones can now be drawn
together. For Paul, the righteousness of God has been revealed,
according to God's own promises, in the appearance of his Messiah,
Jesus. God's righteousness is a power that effects salvation apart from
the law. It is God's right-wising power. In spite of human rebellion
and sin, God has acted to restore fallen humanity to himself purely
by his grace and love. This act of righteousness has been carried out
in the death and resurrection of God's Son, Jesus. In the crucifixion
God has provided a "mercy seat" once and for all. The cross is a
demonstration of the divine love and righteousness. The crucified
Christ is the one who bears the divine condemnation upon sin, but
at the same time this is not a means by which God is placated (or
propitiated). The mercy seat has been provided by God himself; in
Christ God was reconciling the world to himself, not counting
human trepasses any longer, and thereby demonstrating his righteousness. From this act of God — concretely manifested in the obedience of Jesus — there flows justification and life for all humanity.
God justifies the ungodly.

The justification of humanity, however, is revealed only through
the gospel, the good news of what God has done. It will be revealed

to all at the final judgment when God will finally be "everything to everyone." But already in the present age God's justifying power is declared through the gospel. It is realized proleptically whenever and wherever the gospel is heard and believed. Those who accept the good news enjoy the eschatological gift of justification already, even while living in the present age. They have become a part of the new creation, the age to come, and live in the certainty that nothing in all creation, nor even things to come, can separate them from the love of God in Christ. They are the saved, living in the midst of a world whose form is perishing and doomed to pass away. They differ from unbelievers not in the sense that they alone are saved and that unbelievers are condemned. They differ rather in the sense that that which is in store for the whole created order, including humanity that does not know the gospel or even rejects it now, has been granted to them proleptically. They do not therefore boast in their status but rejoice in it and await final redemption.

Paul carried on a mission as an apostle to the gentile nations not simply because he had good news to share, but because he had been commissioned to do so. Since the redemptive work of God in Christ is cosmic in scope, and since peoples of all the nations are to enter into the final glory to come, Paul conceived of his mission as world-embracing. The church on earth must mirror that which is to come. A gospel and mission for the Jews alone, or that requires circumcision and keeping the law on the part of gentiles (in effect, conversion first to Judaism) as a precondition, is incomplete and, in effect, a denial of the gospel itself. The new age, which has already dawned with the resurrection of Jesus Christ from the dead, is the messianic kingdom, and that kingdom includes in principle all the nations in its scope, as the eschatological promises of the prophets declared it would. But for it to include all the nations in fact prior to the Parousia, a mission has to be carried on among the nations. It is unlikely, in light of his expectation of the Parousia imminently, that Paul thought that all persons everywhere—Jew and gentile alike—would hear and believe the gospel. But he set out to proclaim the gospel among the gentile nations and thereby establish congregations among them as the "first fruits" of the new creation. Or to use other cultic language, Paul could speak of his work as rendering a priestly service, preparing an offering, acceptable to God (even if not acceptable to the church at Jerusalem), consisting of believers from among the nations, representative of all the inhabitants of the world. The unity of all humankind in Christ, which will come into its own at the Parousia, is thus being initiated at the dawn of the new age. That unity consists of gentiles from all the nations along with the church at Jerusalem, the earliest and foremost community in Christ. In Paul's view that principle had to be demonstrated even to the Jerusalem community itself.

Paul's collection from his gentile congregations for the church at Jerusalem was one way to symbolize the unity. But in addition and prior to that, Paul went on a course from Jerusalem north and west, hoping to go as far as Spain and perhaps beyond, to establish congregations where Christ had not already been named. By so doing, he was able to act out his conviction that in Christ God had reconciled the world to himself, and that the era between the resurrection and the Parousia was the time allotted to him as apostle to usher in the first stage of the ingathering of the nations under the lordship of Christ. The procession of the nations into the kingdom must begin, and the risen Christ had commissioned him to start that procession. Paul's theology and mission therefore cohere—not in the sense that his mission simply flows from his theology, but in the sense that his theology is a mission theology. The eschatological promises of the prophets concerning the nations—that they too will know the Lord and enjoy the blessings of the messianic kingdom of peace and unity—have been confirmed in the sending of God's Son for the salvation of the world. It is this good news that gave impetus to Paul's missionary theology, and it is the basis for a missionary theology in every age.

NOTES

1. Martin Dibelius, "Paulus und die Mystik," in *Botschaft und Geschichte: Gesammelte Aufsätze* (Tübingen: J. C. B. Mohr [Paul Siebeck], 1953–56), 2:158; Johannes Munck, *Paul and the Salvation of Mankind* (Atlanta: John

Knox Press, 1959), 24–35; Walter Schmithals, *The Office of Apostle in the Early Church* (Nashville: Abingdon Press, 1969), 24–31; Krister Stendahl, *Paul among Jews and Gentiles* (Philadelphia: Fortress Press, 1976), 7–11; and J. Christiaan Beker, *Paul the Apostle: The Triumph of God in Life and Thought* (Philadelphia: Fortress Press, 1980), 3–11. For a study that speaks in terms of conversion, see J. G. Gager, "Some Notes on Paul's Conversion," *NTS* 27 (1981):697–704.

2. Cf. Ferdinand Hahn, *Mission in the New Testament*, SBT 47 (Naperville, Ill.: Alec R. Allenson, 1965), 97–98; and Heinrich Kasting, *Die Anfänge der urchristlichen Mission: Eine historische Untersuchung*, BEvT 55 (Munich: Chr. Kaiser, 1969), 56–60.

3. The concept of "nations" is traditional long before Paul. In Genesis 10 (the so-called table of nations) the peoples of the world are differentiated by languages, families, lands, and "nations" (10:5, 20, 31–32).

4. C. K. Barrett, *A Commentary on the Second Epistle to the Corinthians*, HNTC (New York: Harper & Row, 1973), 268–69.

5. Concerning estimates of the size of the Jewish population in Antioch of Syria in proportion to the much larger gentile population, see Wayne A. Meeks and Robert L. Wilken, *Jews and Christians in Antioch in the First Four Centuries of the Common Era*, SBLSBS 13 (Missoula, Mont.: Scholars Press, 1978), 8.

6. John Knox, "Romans 15:14–33 and Paul's Conception of His Apostolic Mission," *JBL* 83 (1964):10.

7. Cf. Günther Bornkamm, *Paul* (New York: Harper & Row, 1971), 39; Hans Dieter Betz, *Galatians*, Hermeneia (Philadelphia: Fortress Press, 1979), 100; E. P. Sanders, *Paul, the Law, and the Jewish People* (Philadelphia: Fortress Press, 1983), 186.

8. Cf. W. D. Davies, *Paul and Rabbinic Judaism: Some Rabbinic Elements in Pauline Theology*, 4th ed. (Philadelphia: Fortress Press, 1980), 68.

9. Cf. Günther Bornkamm, *Paul* (New York: Harper & Row, 1971), 39–40.

10. "Gentiles" is the rendering in major studies: Ernest DeWitt Burton, *A Critical and Exegetical Commentary on the Epistle to the Galatians*, ICC (New York: Charles Scribner's Sons, 1928), 53; Betz, *Galatians*, 72; and Munck, *Paul and the Salvation of Mankind*, 26.

11. Georg Bertram, "*Ethnos*," *TDNT*, 2:368.

12. Ibid.

13. Cf. also Sir. 44:19.

14. Cf. also Sir. 44:21.

15. There is a tendency to place greater stress on "the nations" in the LXX of Deutero-Isaiah than in the MT, according to John W. Olley, "*Righteousness" in the Septuagint of Isaiah: A Contextual Study*, SBLSCS 8 (Missoula, Mont.: Scholars Press, 1979), 147–51.

16. Many texts of the rabbinic literature are cited by Ulrich Wilckens, *Der Brief an die Römer*, EKKNT 6 (Köln: Benziger; Neukirchen-Vluyn: Neukirchener, 1978–82), 2:255, n. 1145.

17. Munck, *Paul and the Salvation of Mankind*, 51–53.

18. Cf. Dieter Georgi, *Die Geschichte der Kollekte des Paulus für Jerusalem*, TF 38 (Hamburg-Bergstedt: H. Reich Theologischer Verlag, 1965); Bornkamm, *Paul*, 41; Bengt Holmberg, *Paul and Power: The Structure of Authority in the Primitive Church as Reflected in the Pauline Epistles*, ConBNT 11 (Lund: C. W. K. Gleerup, 1978), 35–43; Keith F. Nickle, *The Collection: A Study in Paul's Strategy*, SBT 48 (London: SCM Press, 1966); Munck, *Paul and the Salvation of Mankind*, 287–97; and Wilckens, *Römer*, 3:124–25.

19. Nor does Paul regard the Roman congregation as lacking an "apostolic foundation" or the "fundamental kerygma," as suggested by Günther Klein, "Paul's Purpose in Writing the Epistle to the Romans," in *The Romans Debate*, ed. Karl Donfried (Minneapolis: Augsburg Pub. House, 1977), 32–49 (see esp. pp. 44, 48).

20. William Sanday and Arthur C. Headlam, *A Critical and Exegetical Commentary on the Epistle to the Romans*, 5th ed., ICC (Edinburgh: T. & T. Clark, 1902), 407; Ernst Käsemann, *Commentary on Romans* (Grand Rapids: Wm. B. Eerdmans, 1980), 394; Bornkamm, *Paul*, 53; C. E. B. Cranfield, *A Critical and Exegetical Commentary on the Epistle to the Romans*, ICC (Edinburgh: T. & T. Clark, 1975–79), 760–61; and Wilckens, *Römer*, 3:119–20.

21. BAGD, 457.

22. Munck, *Paul and the Salvation of Mankind*, 51–53; cf. also Käsemann, *Romans*, 395.

23. Bornkamm, *Paul*, 53–54.

24. Knox, "Romans 15:14–33 and Paul's Conception of His Apostolic Mission," 11.

25. Cf. Munck, *Paul and the Salvation of Mankind*, 52.

26. Adolf Deissmann, *St. Paul: A Study in Social and Religious History* (London: Hodder & Stoughton, 1912), 41, 88, and the map in the jacket of his book, "The World as Known to Paul."

27. The term *hierougein* "occurs frequently in Philo and Josephus but always in the sense of offering (a sacrifice)," Cranfield, *Romans*, 756; cf. BAGD, 373.

28. Cf. BAGD, 720; Str-B, 3:153; Otto Michel, *Der Brief an die Römer*, 11th ed., MeyerK 4 (Göttingen: Vandenhoeck & Ruprecht, 1957), 328; Käsemann, *Romans*, 393; and Cranfield, *Romans*, 756–57.

29. The appendix to the Nestle-Aland text (26th ed.) lists some twenty-one allusions to Sirach in the seven undisputed letters of Paul. For illustrations, see E. Earle Ellis, *Paul's Use of the Old Testament* (Edinburgh: Oliver & Boyd, 1957), 59, 76, 153.

30. In Isa. 66:20 the reference is to Jews of the Diaspora who will come from the nations, but in Rom. 15:16 it is nations themselves that are in view—perhaps in light of Isa. 66:18, which speaks of gathering "all nations and tongues."

31. Cf. John Murray, *The Epistle to the Romans* (Grand Rapids: Wm. B. Eerdmans, 1959–65), 2:210; Michel, *Römer*, 328; Matthew Black, *Romans*, NCB (Greenwood: Attic, 1973), 175; K. Weiss, "Paulus—Priester der christl. Kultgemeinde," *TLZ* 79 (1954):355–63; and Gordon P. Wiles, *Paul's Intercessory Prayers*, SNTSMS 24 (Cambridge: Cambridge Univ. Press, 1974), 85, n. 5. On the significance of Deutero-Isaiah for Paul's understanding of his apostleship, see Traugott Holtz, "Zum Selbstverständnis des Apostels Paulus," *TLZ* 91 (1966):321–330.

32. So Käsemann, *Romans*, 393.

33. Cf. Adolf Schlatter, *Gottes Gerechtigkeit: Ein Kommentar zum Römerbrief*, 2d ed. (Stuttgart: Calwer, 1952), 386; Michel, *Römer*, 328; U. Luz, *Das Geschichtsverständnis des Paulus*, 392; Cranfield, *Romans*, 757; Wilckens, *Römer*, 3:118; and Martin Hengel, "The Origins of the Christian Mission," in *Between Jesus and Paul: Studies in the Earliest History of Christianity* (Philadelphia: Fortress Press, 1983), 51.

34. Cf. Gerhard Delling, "*Aparchē*," *TDNT*, 1:484–86. Cf. also 2 Cor. 5:5 where Paul uses the synonym "*arrabōn* (first-fruits) of the Spirit." On the latter as a synonym, see BAGD, 109.

35. That Rom. 11:16 refers to Jewish Christians, see C. K. Barrett, *A Commentary on the Epistle to the Romans*, HNTC (New York: Harper & Brothers, 1957), 216; and Cranfield, *Romans*, 564.

36. The passage is found at 2.25 in *ANF*, 7.410.

37. Delling, "*Aparchē*," *TDNT*, 1:485.

38. The term *prosphora* appears only fourteen times in the LXX (nine of which are in Sirach), whereas *aparchē* is used over seventy times. Both terms are used in only two books of the Old Testament: the Psalms and Sirach.

39. Walther Eichrodt, *Theology of the Old Testament* (Philadelphia: Westminster Press, 1961–67), 1:152; Gerhard von Rad, *Old Testament Theology* (New York: Harper & Row, 1962–65), 1:254.

40. Johs. Pedersen, *Israel: Its Life and Culture* (London: Oxford Univ. Press, 1926–40), 2:301.

41. For this translation, rather than "a hardening has come upon part of Israel" (RSV), see Black, *Romans*, 147; cf. NEB.

42. Cranfield, *Romans*, 575; cf. also Murray, *Romans*, 2:93.

43. Cf. Munck, *Paul and the Salvation of Mankind*, 48; idem, *Christ and Israel: An Interpretation of Romans 9 – 11* (Philadelphia: Fortress Press, 1967), 134–35.

44. Peter Stuhlmacher, "Zur Interpretation von Römer 11,25–32," in *Probleme biblischer Theologie*, ed. Hans W. Wolff (Munich: Chr. Kaiser, 1971), 565–66; and Käsemann, *Romans*, 312.

45. Cf. Munck, *Paul and the Salvation of Mankind*, 48; idem, *Christ and Israel*, 134–35.

46. The term "God-fearers" is discussed by Kirsopp Lake, "Proselytes and God-fearers," in *The Beginnings of Christianity*, ed. F. J. Foakes-Jackson and

K. Lake (London: Macmillan & Co., 1920–33), 5:74–96; Karl G. Kuhn, "*Prosēlytos*," *TDNT*, 6:743–44; and Joachim Jeremias, *Jerusalem in the Time of Jesus* (Philadelphia: Fortress Press, 1969), 320.

47. A. D. Nock, *Paul* (New York: Harper & Brothers, 1938), 91–92; W. D. Davies, *Paul and Rabbinic Judaism*, 68; idem, "Paul and the People of Israel," in *Jewish and Pauline Studies*, 135; Kuhn, "*Prosēlytos*," *TDNT*, 6:744; Munck, *Paul and the Salvation of Mankind*, 120; Philipp Vielhauer, "On the 'Paulinism' of Acts," in *Studies in Luke-Acts*, ed. L. E. Keck and J. L. Martyn (Nashville: Abingdon Press, 1966; reprinted, Philadelphia: Fortress Press, 1980), 38–39; Peter Richardson, *Israel in the Apostolic Church*, SNTSMS 10 (Cambridge: Cambridge Univ. Press, 1969), 136; Richard Longenecker, *The Ministry and Message of Paul* (Grand Rapids: Zondervan, 1971), 37–48; John G. Gager, *Kingdom and Community: The Social World of Early Christianity* (Englewood Cliffs, N.J.: Prentice-Hall, 1975), 128; Abraham J. Malherbe, *Social Aspects of Early Christianity* (Baton Rouge, La.: Louisiana State Univ. Press, 1977), 64; Lloyd Gaston, "Paul and the Torah," in *Antisemitism and the Foundations of Christianity*, ed. Alan T. Davies (New York: Paulist Press, 1979), 55–56; Beker, *Paul the Apostle*, 76; and Gerd Theissen, *The Social Setting of Pauline Christianity: Essays on Corinth* (Philadelphia: Fortress Press, 1982), 102–104.

48. A similar term *(theosebēs)* appears at John 9:31.

49. For references in inscriptions, see K. G. Kuhn and H. Stegemann, "Proselyten," *PWSup.*, 9:1248–83; and M. J. Mellink, "Archaeology in Asia Minor," *AJA* 81/3 (1977):305–6. For critique, see A. T. Kraabel, "The Disappearance of the 'God-Fearers,'" *Numen* 28 (1981):113–26.

50. Quoted from *Josephus*, 3.519. Also at *J.W.* 6.427 Josephus refers to "foreigners present for worship"; text in *Josephus*, 3.499.

51. E. P. Sanders, *Paul, the Law, and the Jewish People*, 182–86.

52. Wayne A. Meeks, *The First Urban Christians: The Social World of the Apostle Paul* (New Haven, Conn.: Yale Univ. Press, 1983), 29; Meeks cites the work of Ronald F. Hock, *The Social Context of Paul's Ministry: Tentmaking and Apostleship* (Philadelphia: Fortress Press, 1980). It should be noted, however, that Meeks does not discount the view that some members of the Pauline congregations were from the God-fearers; in fact he affirms it (p. 73 and elsewhere).

53. Cf. Werner G. Kümmel, *Introduction to the New Testament*, rev. ed. (Nashville: Abingdon Press, 1975), 271.

54. Flogging was a means of discipline for various offenses, including rebelliousness against synagogue authority. See *m. Sanh.* 1.2; K. Kohler, "Synagogue," in *Dictionary of the Apostolic Church*, ed. J. Hastings (New York: Charles Scribner's Sons, 1916–22), 2:545; L. N. Dembitz, "Stripes," in *Jewish Encyclopedia*, ed. I. Singer (New York: Funk and Wagnalls, 1901–06), 11:570; J. Juster, *Les Juifs dans l'empire romaine* (Paris: Guenther, 1914), 2:161–62; H. Mantel, *Studies in the History of the Sanhedrin*, Harvard

Semitic Studies 17 (Cambridge, Mass.: Harvard Univ. Press, 1965), 295; H. H. Cohn, "Bet Din and Judges," *EncJud*, 4:720–21; and Arland J. Hultgren, "Paul's Pre-Christian Persecutions of the Church: Their Purpose, Locale, and Nature," *JBL* 95 (1976):104.

55. For a review of the discussion and a defense of its authenticity, see W. D. Davies, "Paul and the People of Israel," 124–27; and I. Howard Marshall, *1 and 2 Thessalonians*, NCB (Grand Rapids: Wm. B. Eerdmans, 1983), 11–12.

56. Birger A. Pearson, "1 Thessalonians 2:13–16: A Deutero-Pauline Interpolation," *HTR* 64 (1971):79–94; Daryl Schmidt, "1 Thess. 2:13–16: Linguistic Evidence for an Interpolation," *JBL* 102 (1983): 269–79; and others (see survey by Schmidt).

57. That the "countrymen" would refer to Jewish (not simply gentile) persecutors is held by James E. Frame, *A Critical and Exegetical Commentary on the Epistles of Paul to the Thessalonians*, ICC (Edinburgh: T. & T. Clark, 1912), 109; A. L. Moore, *1 and 2 Thessalonians*, NCB (Camden, N.J.: Thomas Nelson & Sons, 1969), 44; and Marshall, *1 and 2 Thessalonians*, 78–79.

58. Cf. Juvenal, *Satires* 14.96–106. Cf. also G. F. Moore, *Judaism*, 1:325; and Eduard Lohse, *The New Testament Environment* (Nashville: Abingdon Press, 1976), 125.

59. Sanders, *Paul, the Law, and the Jewish People*, 186.

60. Ibid., 185.

61. Ibid., 188.

62. Ibid., 185–87.

63. Ibid., 188.

64. Cf. Meeks, *First Urban Christians*, 84–107, who provides a description of the social cohesion of the Pauline churches in light of the apostle's theological emphases (esp. pp. 92 and 97).

65. Cf. Günther Bornkamm, "The Missionary Stance of Paul in I Corinthians 9 and in Acts," in *Studies in Luke-Acts*, ed. L. E. Keck and J. L. Martyn, 200.

Index of
Ancient Sources

Where references are to notes, the numbers of these are given in parentheses after the page numbers.

Index of
Modern Authors

Where references are to notes, the numbers of these are given in parentheses after the page numbers.

158